# PRAISE

"*Iterate* presents one of the most notably unique, boldly original, and common-sensically practical approaches to managing teams to come along in years. Through the clever use of story, Ed Muzio walks you through scenario after scenario of how to take each reasonable, logical next step toward organizational success. He describes what to do and provides an entire kit of practical tools and videos to help you succeed. It's a comprehensive curriculum for mastering management in an entirely new way."

—**JIM KOUZES,** COAUTHOR OF *THE LEADERSHIP CHALLENGE*
AND THE DEAN'S EXECUTIVE FELLOW OF LEADERSHIP,
LEAVEY SCHOOL OF BUSINESS, SANTA CLARA UNIVERSITY

"Leaders feel pressure to make sure everything gets done but also empower and develop their people. Ed brings these opposite forces together with clear guidance that keeps the whole group performing yet ensures each individual will take responsibility for the big picture. Whether you lead a management team yourself or coach someone who does, *Iterate* is a must-read to get everyone going in the right direction—and the *same* direction—every step of the way."

—**MARSHALL GOLDSMITH,** AUTHOR OF THE #1 NEW YORK TIMES
BEST SELLER, *TRIGGERS*

"*Iterate* is about the real work of managing managers. Ed Muzio's message is clear and necessary in today's working world—and it is delivered in each chapter through a diverse team of managers, each with unique and relatable behaviors, tasks, and styles. As entertaining as it is enlightening, *Iterate* will appeal to management teams everywhere."

—**KEN BLANCHARD,** COAUTHOR OF *THE NEW ONE MINUTE MANAGER*®
AND *SERVANT LEADERSHIP IN ACTION*

"Our organizations are complex systems. To find success, smart managers must iterate, embracing that complexity rather than wishing it would all go away. This book helps managers break through and lift their leadership and their teams to a new level."

—**MICHAEL BUNGAY STANIER,** AUTHOR OF *THE COACHING HABIT*

"*Iterate* provides a great framework for running an organization with speed and efficiency. It eliminates politics, it's easy to implement, and it works even when implemented informally. Muzio's interactive management model creates teams that are self-developing, which benefits the organization in the long run."

—**LAURA OLIPHANT**, CEO, TRANSLARITY

"A must-read for managers who want to improve performance and achieve not only great results but also *the right results* consistently over time. What sets *Iterate* apart from other books on management and leadership is its focus on the organization—and on the specific management practices and behaviors that make the organization perform. If 'fast, flexible, and focused' sounds like the right prescription for your management team, read this book and learn to *Iterate!*"

—**DAVID C. SMITH**, LEADERSHIP & ORGANIZATIONAL DEVELOPMENT, NASA JET PROPULSION LABORATORY

"*Iterate* will change the way managers show up for work and move all of management into a more effective zone. Muzio's laser focus on conveying information, making adjustments, and keeping everyone apprised in real time will add a new level of nimbleness to your team and deepen your own understanding of what's going on in your organization."

—**KAREN ALDERMAN**, DIRECTOR OF HUMAN RESOURCES AND ADMINISTRATION, YALE LAW SCHOOL

"Iterative Management is to traditional organizational management what Agile was to traditional project management: the next evolutionary step that could be the difference between survival and extinction. In this book, Muzio has woven together virtually every management best practice I can recall from 35 years of working with great managers in a variety of world-class organizations. Whether the organization you manage is large or small, you need Iterative Management."

—**ROB SHAUM**, CERTIFIED LEAN SIX SIGMA MASTER BLACK BELT AND SENIOR DIRECTOR OF DATA SCIENCE, CHILDREN'S HEALTH SYSTEM OF TEXAS

"*Iterate* doesn't belong at the top of your stack of business books—it belongs in your hands during your next coffee break! In an easy, thought-provoking read, Muzio explains how to best manage managers and why doing so is imperative. This is a rarely-addressed topic in management development, and you'll understand it in a whole new way."

—**DAWN ADAMS MILLER**, SENIOR L&D SPECIALIST, ORACLE

"*Iterate* is a winner—and required reading for my whole team managing 1,200 individual contributors. Muzio cuts through the noise and addresses the realities of the business world with well-defined and well-researched solutions. This book is a field guide to running a high-performing organization *and* an MBA management course, all in one."

—**BRENT BLOOM**, VICE PRESIDENT,
SERVICE OPERATIONS & TRAINING, APPLIED MATERIALS

"Backed by decades of research, Muzio turns traditional management thinking on its head and gives you practical examples for a better way to run your organization. The *aha* moments in this book are endless, and the advice is clear and simple."

—**CHERIE BROTHERS**, HR ANALYST, GOVERNMENT ORGANIZATION

"Muzio has developed practical, straightforward approaches for tackling some of the workplace's thorniest issues—and he provides the tools, charts, and worksheets needed to begin. Ed's methodology will help both experienced and new managers get better at communicating, planning, and executing on their plans. *Iterate* is an easy read for leaders and managers at every level, and it will leave you feeling better equipped to run your management team, starting right now."

—**CATHY BROWN**, SR. PROGRAM MANAGER, INSTRUCTIONAL ARCHITECT,
INSTITUTE OF NUCLEAR POWER OPERATIONS

"*Iterate* provides a great structure for creating a continuous learning organization. Muzio's Five Key Practices describe essential behaviors for successful management and leadership in today's work environment, and his reflection callouts are really helpful in the application of those practices."

—**ED CLEARY**, PROGRAM MANAGER, FORTUNE 100 FINANCIAL SERVICES COMPANY

"*Iterate* is the best articulation of everything we know about management and management meetings."

—**BILL DANIELS**, CEO, AMERICAN CONSULTING AND TRAINING

"Muzio offers outstanding insight into how managers succeed in the fast-paced, networked organizations of our modern economy. *Iterate* offers practical, measurable ways to ensure management and knowledge workers hit their targets. If you're a manager, you have something to gain from the techniques in this book."

—**STEVE FEYER**, PRODUCT MARKETING DIRECTOR, APTTUS

"*Iterate* shows managers how to define the rules of their game, keep score, and make 'in game adjustments' that lead to victories. Muzio blends timeless and timely management thought into a cogent framework for articulating, aligning, assessing, and achieving organizational goals and provides a robust portfolio of tools to help readers make the leap from theory to practice."

—**CAMERON M. FORD**, PHD, DIRECTOR, CENTER FOR ENTREPRENEURIAL LEADERSHIP, EXECUTIVE DIRECTOR, BLACKSTONE LAUNCHPAD AT UCF, COLLEGE OF BUSINESS ADMINISTRATION, UNIVERSITY OF CENTRAL FLORIDA

"*Iterate* is the starting point to address—or even better, avoid—organizational challenges like competing priorities, lack of alignment, and fuzzy accountability. If you can master the key practices and core components, you'll have a culture of agility, honesty, execution, and continuous learning. Muzio has created a guidebook to your organization's success."

—**DR. ILEAN GALLOWAY**, EXECUTIVE DIRECTOR, ORGANIZATION DEVELOPMENT & LEARNING, EISAI INC.

"*Iterate* is based on the psychology of how people work together. It keeps the focus on real behaviors instead of general labels and is full of practical tools and tips. You'll feel smarter and be better equipped to manage people after reading it."

—**STEPHANIE HEMMERT**, SENIOR EDUCATION ATTORNEY, FEDERAL GOVERNMENT AGENCY

"Research proves that writing effective business goals is difficult; managing teams to execute those goals is just as challenging. In these turbulent, complex times, managers need a system to broadcast status, preview results, and make decisions that keep their teams in sync with the organization. Ed Muzio's *Iterate* provides that system: It's clear, it's executable, and frankly, it's 'SMART as Hell'—I wish I had written it!"

—**GLENN HUGHES**, AWARD-WINNING AUTHOR OF
*A GRAPHIC GUIDE TO WRITING SMART AS HELL GOALS!*

"*Iterate* provides practical management tools to break down complexity and help you adapt quickly to today's fast-paced business environment. Ed's focus on inclusive behaviors and functional conversations equips managers and their teams to stay ahead of the curve and deliver."

—**SUSAN INSLEY**, VICE PRESIDENT OF HUMAN RESOURCES, VMWARE

"Muzio is one of the planet's clearest thinkers on management practice."

—**HELEN KELLY**, EUROPEAN EDITOR, *THE WORKING MANAGER*

"As an executive leader with over 25 years of experience spanning multiple C-level roles in product management and engineering, customer experience, and information technology, I have read dozens of books on leadership and management. *Iterate* is the clearest method I've seen for creating and leading a management team that handles complexity without becoming rigid—Muzio's advice is practical and targeted. Because my company's focus on innovation demands that we stay focused yet adaptable amidst rapid change, I am handing out copies of *Iterate* to my own senior leadership team. Take a look, read the book, and I guarantee you'll have your enterprise running better before you finish the last chapter!"

—**BRIAN LILLIE**, CHIEF PRODUCT OFFICER, EQUINIX

"As our company grew from less than 50 people to more than 400, we faced significant challenges in sustaining efficient information flow throughout our organization and coordinating fast, effective decision making. Iterative Management gave us the tools to address these challenges successfully, so that we could scale rapidly while maintaining our market leadership position and our reputation for innovation and agility. We highly recommended this approach for any emerging company that needs to scale quickly."

—**CONOR MADIGAN**, PHD, PRESIDENT AND CO-FOUNDER, KATEEVA

"Deceptively simple, actionable, and comprehensive, this book is a clearly laid-out guide to the discipline of managing management that's useful for all levels, including the most senior leaders. Consistently practicing the key elements Muzio outlines will eliminate counterproductive 'organizational blast waves' that often have significant negative consequences. *Iterate* is a call to action that will change your people, products, and profits."

—**PAUL MARELLA**, SENIOR DIRECTOR, CORPORATE LEARNING CENTER AND FORMER SENIOR VICE PRESIDENT & DIVISION GENERAL MANAGER, KLA-TENCOR

"As an HR professional with over two decades of experience in supporting managers, I highly recommend *Iterate*. It not only offers us a chance to deal with the talent shortage we all face by boosting our teams and the individuals who make them up but also is a comprehensive, tactical toolkit that enables management teams to optimize their systems, processes, and organizations. I loved it!"

—**VAADRA MARTINEZ**, DIRECTOR OF HUMAN RESOURCES, LAVU INC.

"This book raises the manager and team performance bar up—way up! Muzio covers complex concepts in a conversational language that's not only easy to understand but also specific enough to put into practice. You'll be able to apply the tools and advice immediately, and at any level. *Iterate* is going on my team's required reading list."

—**SUSAN PAVELEK**, MANAGER, BUSINESS PROCESS MANAGEMENT, OCCIDENTAL PETROLEUM CORPORATION

"Throw out HR's traditional 'performance management' and manage *business performance* instead. Lead your people as Muzio outlines, and you'll create a regular cadence of adaptation that keeps both management and the front line ahead of the next change instead of constantly chasing after the last one."

—**BRETT RODGERS**, VICE PRESIDENT OF
GLOBAL HUMAN RESOURCES, SACHEM, INC.

"Founded on well-established principles of organizational learning and developed over years of consulting experience, this book presents a packaged system of practical methods to help managers deal with uncertainty. *Iterate* is a valuable, reliable resource for any manager who's looking for tools to manage successfully in a complex world."

—**CARL SCHUH**, JD & RETIRED INSTRUCTOR, HUGH DOWNS SCHOOL OF
HUMAN COMMUNICATION, ARIZONA STATE UNIVERSITY

"Muzio has been in the trenches, and it shows. *Iterate* provides immediate, easy-to-implement advice, supported by vivid illustrations and clear examples. You'll improve your communication and strengthen your management team as soon as you start reading."

—**DENISE SCHULTZE**, BUSINESS EXCELLENCE MANAGER, PLASMA-THERM, LLC

"The pace of change and disruption facing organizations is unlikely to ever slow down. Whether you're in a large, multinational corporation or a growing start-up, *Iterate* arms your managers with the essential behaviors and practices for learning together to produce results, along with the refreshing openness of a system of management that strives to continuously understand, assess, and improve upon those outcomes. Put these practices in place, *Iterate*, and win!"

—**LEE SESSIONS**, MANAGING DIRECTOR, INTEL CAPITAL

"Are you weary of the corporate tyranny holding you to your predictions of an unpredictable future? Be a force in ending it by implementing the management lessons offered in *Iterate*. Like the best teacher you ever had, Muzio convinces you of your own ability to convert a rigid culture of political competition to one of flexible cooperation in the real world of resource constraints and constant change. His advice is practical, logical, and clear, and you'll know you can do this!"

"Ed has done it again. *Iterate* is a must-read for anyone in a management position or advancing into one. This book breaks down complex concepts and useful tools into simple, actionable illustrations and advice. You'll come away with a thorough understanding of your role in the management system and what you can do to improve your part of the organization."

"Easy-to-read, thought-provoking, and practical. *Iterate* is one of those books you wish you had come across earlier in your career. Muzio's effective illustrations and wise guidance will help anyone, from seasoned executives to brand new managers, improve upon how their teams create plans, make decisions, and deliver results."

# ITERATE

# ITERATE

### RUN A FAST, FLEXIBLE, FOCUSED MANAGEMENT TEAM

## ED MUZIO

AN INC.
ORIGINAL

Group Harmonics, Inc., claims the exclusive right to use "Iterate," "Iterative Management," and the family of "Iterative" marks in connection with business consulting goods and services.

*An Inc. Original*
New York, New York
www.inc.com

Distributed by Greenleaf Book Group

For ordering information or special discounts for bulk purchases, please contact Greenleaf Book Group at PO Box 91869, Austin, TX 78709, 512.891.6100.

Design and composition by Greenleaf Book Group
Cover design by Greenleaf Book Group

Publisher's Cataloging-in-Publication data is available.

Print ISBN: 978-0-9991913-1-6

eBook ISBN: 978-0-9991913-2-3

Part of the Tree Neutral® program, which offsets the number of trees consumed in the production and printing of this book by taking proactive steps, such as planting trees in direct proportion to the number of trees used: www.treeneutral.com

TreeNeutral

Printed in China on acid-free paper

18 19 20 21 22 23 24   10 9 8 7 6 5 4 3 2 1

First Edition

*For Bill and Lila, the giants on whose shoulders I stand.*
*And for Vivian and Zachary, who give me a boost.*

Clear
Output Goals

Verbalized
Summary Outputs

Pragmatic
Dashboards

Consistent
Meeting Rhythm

Self-Managed
Feedback

**OUTPUT & STATUS
BROADCASTING**

Forward Looking
Orientation

Control of
Resources

**FRONT LINE
SELF-SUFFICIENCY**

**WORK PREVIEW
MEETINGS**

Resource
Allocation Focus

it·er·ate℠

Fair-Day's-Work
Forecasts

OSIR Structure
(Non-Narrative)

**LINKED
TEAMS**

**GROUP
DECISION-MAKING**

Upward Looking
Success

Group
Consultative Process

Managers
as Links

Fully Commissioned
Decisions

Interdependent
Approach

100%
Implementation

Continuous
Lateral Development

Disciplined
Meeting Management

# CONTENTS

# PREFACE

Why write yet *another* book about management? Because despite all that has been written already, we still labor under the collective hallucination that the management of managers is no different from the management of individual contributors—that management at any level is nothing more than some vague combination of *getting people to do things* and *getting people to collaborate*. If a manager gets involved in how his or her reports manage, it goes no further than that; any notion of a need for consistency *between* subordinate managers is similarly abstracted into platitudes about results and collaboration.

Every day, people are promoted into middle management and into the ranks of executive management without any deep understanding of what the function entails and with no discussion of how the rest of the management team has collectively decided to perform it. As a result, the majority of business runs on what I call the North American Management Model, an assortment of those platitudes that includes "Do what you see fit to get the work done," "Keep your nose in your own business," "Don't let yourself get pushed around by other interests," and "It's better when we work together." These conflicting banalities aren't wholly incorrect, but they tell only a small part of the story, confusing as much as they clarify.

To the extent that anyone tries to go deeper, we assume that research-based tools for goal-setting, collaboration, teamwork, and decision-making apply within management exactly as they would within any other group of people trying to solve a problem.

They don't.

Managers have a much broader charter than whatever issue they're working on at the moment. They have a complex history and future together that doesn't allow truly independent action and can't be re-created in experiments on group behavior. They're constantly asked to figure out how to do things that haven't been done before, typically given fewer resources than they need to guarantee quality results, and frequently blamed for not foreseeing problems that could only have been obvious in hindsight. They also have all the failings and flaws of regular human beings, who are naturally change averse, territorial, and defensive—especially under stress. And managers are almost always under stress.

If I had my way, there would be a sort of fairy godparent of management who would appear to managers immediately upon each successive advancement. "Congratulations!" my magical messenger would exclaim. "Now that your boss has taken care of the administrative part of your promotion, I'm here to endow you with the *authority* that comes with it. I hereby vest you with a portion of the organization's resources, which may include people, money, equipment, and/or materials. Whatever it is, your organization's aim is to apply those resources intelligently in the pursuit of its goals—which means it's now *your* job to do so. Here's how: Your resources are at their most useful—and your organization is at its most successful—when you and your fellow managers are making coordinated, difficult trade-offs between attractive, high-value uses of them. As a result, you now exist in a constant state of both cooperation with and opposition to the other managers in your organization. Work with them—and push back on them—to constantly solve and solve again the problem of *what to do with the resources under your collective control.*"

My enchanted emissary would then go on to read all of the content of appendix 5 as an explanation of "how we expect you to behave as one of our managers"—and then disappear, presumably, into a puff of smoke.

Unfortunately, no such magical mentor exists. In its absence, this book is a guide to the real work of management and a three-part revelation for those running teams of managers and those who advise them.

First, management is *supposed to be* difficult—not just because getting people to do things is difficult and not just because getting people to collaborate is difficult but because the actual purpose of management is to perform an essential function for the organization that is inherently difficult.

Second, managers shouldn't feel embarrassed or inadequate if they're struggling. The work is legitimately difficult, and worse, it's unlikely that anyone has ever explained to them what management is really about or how to thrive or even survive at it.

Third, absent my magical fairy godparent, it's up to every person who runs a management team to articulate the purpose of management, set consistent expectations for how his or her subordinate managers should perform the function, and communicate and reinforce those expectations with everyone.

Throughout the book, we'll be talking about the traditional challenges of management, too: getting people to do things and getting people to collaborate. We'll have to, because those are part and parcel of the job. But what we're really doing here is shattering our collective illusion that they're the whole story. The rest of it—the set of behaviors of a management team that *understands its own purpose* and *performs it well*—is a great secret known only to the highest-performing organizations. Often, it's only "known," even to them, unconsciously—as unspoken behavioral patterns enshrouded in the ether of their culture.

It's time to snap out of our trance, rub our eyes, and see management clearly—maybe for the first time.

# ACKNOWLEDGMENTS

In some ways, a book is a lie. You hold it in your hands or see it on your screen: a whole package bearing a single name. The message is "The author made this."

As the guy whose name is on the front, I beg to differ. This book would not be possible without a whole village of people and a whole career's worth of experiences, all of which are far too many to list in a simple acknowledgments section. Nevertheless, please allow me to try.

William R. Daniels (Bill) has been a mentor, adviser, and friend for two decades. He was literally the first person I ever asked for advice about becoming a consultant, and his response in that moment was telling: he sat down to lunch with me, a twenty-something engineer, and casually handed over advice that it would take me years to appreciate completely. Over the years since, our relationship evolved to the point where I took over his business upon his retirement. I still call him regularly for advice. Together with his wife and business partner, Lila Sparks-Daniels, Bill has patiently taught me much of what I know about management, most of what I know about management consulting, and quite a bit of what I know about mutually beneficial adult relationships. This book would not exist without their work. My business and my professional career would not exist without their support. And my son's life would be the poorer without their presence as honorary grandparents.

Speaking of my business, creating something this complex robbed time and attention from multiple other projects. Luckily for me, Jennifer Cunningham and Jeanne Wood have been consistent stars on my team—ready, willing, and able to pick up my slack so that I could keep going on *Iterate* without penalizing our enterprise or our clients. They also got roped into advice sessions and discussions ranging from editorial issues to publicity approaches, and they did it all with good humor and excitement about the prize at the end of the race. On another side of the equation, Dave Grenier and Jerry Smith have been invaluable as advisers and creators of the product and internet content that supports this book, and their help has extended beyond simply accomplishing objectives to encouraging me to see what else could be possible. You can't assign a numerical value to that kind of backup.

Of course, the creation and distribution of the book is an art and science in itself. I feel tremendously fortunate to have worked in collaboration with An Inc. Original's publication team at Greenleaf Book Group, which handled everything from editing to cover design to distribution. The list of names includes Justin Branch, Tyler LeBleu, Jessica Choi, Joan Tapper, Sarah Hudgens, Pam Nordberg, Rachael Brandenburg, Corrin Foster, and Kristine Peyre-Ferry—to cite a few. Each of these people played an important role, and behind them were others whom I never met, quietly supporting the effort. I'm also indebted to my friend and fellow author Gary DePaul for pointing me in this amazing team's direction in the first place, to David Ratner, Cathy Lewis, and their team for working tirelessly on media outreach and publicity, and to Daniel Wolf for the design help with the graphic at the center of the work.

And then there's the list of colleagues and clients at every level and from around the globe who have trusted me enough to let me play in their sandboxes, advise their leadership, and learn from and influence their professional worlds. In alphabetical order: Michelle Ajuria, Amy Baker, Suzan Barghash, Brent Bloom, Madonna Bolano, Kishore Bubna, Doug Carpenter, Pedro Cerecer, Audrey Charles, Heidi Clark, Patrick Crow, Karina Daldegan, Juliana Decastro, Gary Dickerson, Santiago Durante, Steve Feyer, Margaret Fiorentino, Nataliya Fleshler, Silvia Furlan, Marie Gabriel, Paul Gaffney, Mike Gilbert, Dave Gonzalez, Lisa Gross, Brian Haas, Alain Harrus, Glen Hawk, Mike Hill, Beate Hillebrecht, Tristan Holtam, Glenn Hughes, Susan Insley, Terese Kemble, Stacy Kirby, Sanjiv Kumar, Esther Liang, Brian Lillie, Jessica Luttrull, Conor Madigan, Missy Madrid, Paul Marella, Patricia Miron, Rand Newby, Ai Nguyen, Laura Oliphant, Steve Overcashier, Scott

Overson, Charlie Pappis, Susan Pavelek, Dan Pond, Mark Retzer, Jeff Rittichier, Brett Rodgers, Nuria Root, Maria Robinson, Rafael Santos, Ron Sacchi, Paige Sacks, Ali Salehpour, Mark Shaw, Sandra Silva, Kevin Slaughter, Dave Smith, Maria Smithson, Esther Stone, Matt Tavlin, Leroy Tucker, John Van Camp, Pamela Walik, Ken Wells, Matt Wokas, JD Wysong, and Fontane Yeung. It's a long list but woefully incomplete; it should by rights include dozens of others, who I hope will forgive my oversight.

It's also worth mentioning that *Iterate* itself started not as a book but as the collection of videos that make up the online class available at **IterateNow.com**. Glenn Hughes's encouragement in creating that class, Mike Gilbert's help developing it, Kishore Bubna's recommendations around positioning it, and Judy Safern's push to make the leap from class to book were instrumental in bringing this project to fruition. Equally important, though less obvious, have been Marianne Wilman, who taught me over the years to be as articulate as possible on camera, and Jeff Miller and his studio team—Chris Eldridge, Steve Kern, Alex Minas, and Doug Wells, whose production and editing have made me appear more articulate in the videos than I probably am in real life.

There's another aspect to what I know about Iterative Management, and that's personal experience in highly effective organizations. Though some years have passed, I feel compelled to acknowledge Intel Corporation and my phenomenal bosses there as the place where I "grew up" professionally. It was a great place to work and a great place to learn. I've been gone more than a decade, but I still give a nod of thanks—a salute to my alma mater—each time I pass the headquarters. That happens, also, to be where I met Bill and Lila Daniels, as well as a number of other friends and colleagues with whom I'm still in touch today.

Last but definitely not least, I must admit that my fascination (or perhaps obsession) with this project has found its way home. I'm grateful to my wife, Vivian, for listening to me talk about "the book" in all its various stages and to my son, Zach, for forcing me to talk about other things (like zombies). I'm also grateful to my parents, Marie and Ed, for insisting on raising independent thinkers. Every building needs a foundation, and mine is strong.

Saying "thank-you" to all of these amazing people and so many more seems reductive. But it's all I've got.

# it·er·ate

*to take the most logical step from where you are and then to do it again. And again. Iteration is how computers simulate complex systems. It's how humankind got from the Wright Flyer to the Boeing 747. And it's how you walk to your car . . .*

*Take your first step! Visit **IterateNow.com** with the unique code located inside your book jacket, and set up your private access to online resources mentioned throughout the book.*

# CHAPTER 1

# THE BEST NEXT STEP

Success is not final; failure is not fatal.
—WINSTON CHURCHILL

You step out the door of a large building and glance at the time. It's 2:27 p.m. Your next meeting is at three o'clock, and it's a half hour's drive away. So you figure you've got three minutes to get yourself into your car and on the road. You look in the direction of where you parked—well, where you think you parked—and you start walking.

What happens next is probably the least interesting part of your day. Right on schedule, at about two thirty, you drop into your seat, start the car, and drive off the lot. It's an unremarkable event, but what it takes to achieve it is actually pretty sophisticated.

At first glance, it may not seem that way. It may seem that all that's happening is that your brain—your own personal executive office—is setting a goal in the form of an output requirement and a deadline: *get to the car in three minutes*. Then your feet, which are your workforce, carry out your orders.

Right?

Sort of—but there's more to it than that. The process does start with a high-level goal set from "above." But as soon as you start walking, things get complicated. As your feet move across the ground, they must deal with subtle variations in the surface. Is there gravel? Is the ground wet or slippery? Your front line workforce—your foot muscles—compensate without any intervention from management to keep you upright and on track.

Meanwhile, those muscles are dependent on blood oxygen, a resource, to keep going. If they're getting enough, everything is fine. If they're not—maybe the pace is too quick or the surface is too difficult—they request more. That's what we might call an escalation.

The escalation goes first to middle management—your cardiovascular system. In some cases, that system can satisfy the need directly. Your heart pumps a bit harder, and more resources are sent where they're needed. In other situations, the request is too great. Middle management can't handle it, so it gets escalated all the way to the top. The request makes it up to your brain, and you get the message: "Breathe harder or walk slower." And you make a choice.

While the work is going on at the bottom, something else is happening at the top: you're looking where you're going. And up in your executive office, you're processing new information. Maybe you see something in your path—an open hole or a tree—and decide to go around it. Or maybe you notice that you're walking toward the wrong car and you need to change direction.

So along you go. You have information flowing up from the bottom of your metaphorical organization and information flowing down from the top. You have decisions being made at all levels, with escalations when necessary. And you have a whole system—that's a key word, *system*—processing all of the information and decisions for one reason: so that in this moment you take the most reasonable step toward your goal, and then in the next moment you take the next most reasonable step from there.

Let me repeat that: you take the next most reasonable step *from there*. Not the next most reasonable step as you foresee it from here.

In other words, you Iterate.

Really, you have no choice. The total trip to your car may be a few hundred steps, but you can't foresee more than the first five or ten when you start. You can't possibly chart your course completely before you begin. And yet, if every step you take, from the first to the last, isn't the most reasonable and useful one *at that moment*, you'll waste time and energy. After each step is complete, the information that came from it—new information that wasn't available before you took it—must be incorporated into the decision about the next one.

Iteration is the way effective systems solve problems whose solutions are too complex to be predefined. It's how trees take shape as they grow. It's how computers simulate weather, traffic patterns, and aircraft flight. It's how humankind got from the first Wright Flyer to the mass-produced Boeing 747. And it's how you walk to your car.

If you're still not impressed by your trip across the parking lot, let's talk about what *doesn't* happen along the way.

You don't find yourself paralyzed on the sidewalk with your feet awaiting permission from your brain to take the next step because you stepped on a piece of gravel that wasn't in the original plan. You don't stop in the middle of the street for a process debate about left-foot-first versus right-foot-first. You don't see an open manhole coming forty paces away, repeatedly decide to change direction, and then fall down the hole anyway. You don't arrive at the wrong car or arrive 50% to 200% later than you expected (as many business initiatives do). You don't run out of blood oxygen because your foot muscles can't get what they need from your cardiovascular system. And you don't roam the parking lot in circles, trying to decide whether you'll ever get to the car or whether you should cancel your three o'clock meeting.

Any of those outcomes would be, well, dumb. But they don't happen. Not on your walk to the car.

They *do* happen in organizations. Micromanagement from above stalls progress below. Turf wars stifle output. Lack of flexibility makes even the most foreseeable problems impossible to avoid. Plans and budgets never catch up with real complexity and cost. Resources are held hostage by cumbersome approval processes. And lack of information from above and below pollutes decision-making at all levels.

You've probably been part of a "dumb" work group or organization—one that delivered less intelligent decisions and results than those its individual members could have come up with alone. If so, you know how frustrating and wasteful this is.

If you're lucky, you've also been part of a smart organization—one that Iterates. One that moves the right information up and down the hierarchy, in regular and useful ways, in support of good decisions. One that makes good decisions at every level. One that doesn't get stuck in an overly rigid *plan* but instead stays flexible as it pursues clearly defined *outcomes*. One that continually asks itself the question, "What's the next most logical step to be taken?" and then takes it, learns from it, and repeats.

If you've had this experience, you know how engaging and exciting it can be to Iterate—to work in groups that produce a whole lot *more* intelligence together than their members could alone. If you haven't had it, you should know that such places exist. They do, and they're not nearly the minority that you may imagine. Simply look for the highest-performing entrants in any given market space. Chances are they're Iterating.

Whether or not you've experienced such an organization firsthand, you need to know not only that they exist but also that they're consistent and recognizable: they share common behaviors that can be defined, observed, encouraged, and rewarded. In my firm's work with our clients, we rely on more than seventy years of research, information, and experience to define *exactly* what people do in these organizations—especially the people in management. And we have almost that much collective experience helping leaders, managers, and their teams to improve at it. Anyone who runs or advises a management team *without* understanding Iteration is doing both the team and the company a huge disservice.

This book is your guide to running an Iterative organization. It's written with three goals in mind. First, for you to *understand*: to learn the key behaviors of management that make an organization Iterate (and keep it from being dumb). Second, for you to *assess*: to recognize the extent to which those behaviors are present or absent—in yourself as a manager, among the managers you supervise, and in the managers around and above you. And third, for you to *improve*: to help yourself, your team, and your organization to Iterate—even just a little more than they do now.

▶ WATCH THE VIDEO!

Your copy of this book includes prepaid access to a library of videos, including *Iterate—The Walk to Your Car.* You can watch the video now, then return to it later to refresh your memory or share concepts with others. Create your free account and watch any video, anytime, at **IterateNow.com**.

———————— ACTIVITY ————————

Reflect on the extent to which your organization as a whole exhibits Iterative characteristics.

1. How does your organization allow you to repeatedly "take the next most logical step," as in the story of your walk to the car? How does it get in your way?

2. How do *you* allow the organization *you* manage to "take the next most logical step"? How do *you* get in its way?

## Iteration Requires Feedback

The idea of Iteration applies to many natural and man-made systems. A pretty simple one involves the temperature in our homes.

You walk over to the wall and set your thermostat to the temperature you want. Then the air conditioner or heater turns on and off all day long to keep your house at about that temperature.

Now, you might do a lot of thinking about what temperature to set, and if you live with other people, there might be some serious debate about that! But once the number is set, unless something goes wrong, you can pretty much trust that the temperature will stay consistent. A lot of things change throughout the day—the outside temperature, hot sun coming through the windows, cold rain falling on the roof, the number of people inside, and whether anyone is using the stove, to name a few—and yet, the system still gets it right.

It gets it right through Iteration. Think about it: the heating and cooling equipment is an output machine. To act, it needs a simple input—an instruction to turn the heating on, the cooling on, or the system off. With that, it does its work, and it produces output—a change in the temperature or no change, depending on the input.

The thermostat gives *input* to the machinery—not just any input but input intended to drive future *output* in the right direction. It reads the temperature in the house, compares it to the target you set, and determines the next most reasonable step. If the house is warmer than the set point, it switches on the cooling. If the house is colder, it switches on the heating. If the temperature is about right, it switches everything off. And then it checks again.[1]

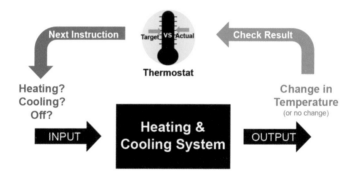

The thermostat provides feedback so that the heating and cooling system can Iterate.

The thermostat, in other words, provides the system with *feedback*. Without it, you'd constantly be too hot or too cold. With it, regular adjustments based on the current situation—what we call Iteration—keep the machinery operating in line with the desired result.

*Iteration requires feedback.*

Remember, Iteration is the way effective systems solve problems whose solutions can't be predefined. There's no way you could sit down on Monday and plan the exact on and off times for your climate-control system all week to deliver a consistent temperature. The system has to Iterate.

---

1 Even if your thermostat requires manual selection of hot or cold, it provides feedback for heating or cooling, as described here.

The same is true for your organization. You can't simply set it in motion and let it go because you can't possibly foresee what it will face—not even in the *near* future. Competitive pressure, technology, customer demands—so much is changing so fast that there's no way to *plan* your way to revenue targets, program launches, or other critical goals in advance. Things change every step of the way.

And this doesn't all come from "out there." Your organization itself creates change as it goes. The release of a new product or service provokes a different market response than expected; the redesign of a business process creates unforeseen impacts on customer service needs; investigation of a possible expansion engenders a surprising response from the existing workforce. Things not only change because they're changing; they also change because *you're changing them.*

Compared with this level of complexity, walking to your car or adjusting the temperature in your house is child's play. Your organization needs to be constantly, effectively monitoring its current state, analyzing current progress to its desired future outcome, and making adjustments. It needs to Iterate.

And Iteration requires feedback.

So what's the organizational equivalent of the thermostat? What's in place to constantly check the output of the machinery against a target and adjust the input accordingly so that broader objectives are reached? What is the feedback system of the organization?

There's actually a one-word answer to that question: *management.* The purpose of management—the core purpose, I would argue—is systemic feedback. If the organization's strategic plan and objectives are what create the set point for the thermostat, and if the organization itself is what creates the heating or cooling, then it's the management team that keeps checking the temperature and adjusting what everyone is doing.

Though often misunderstood, this is why management exists.

Think for a moment: is there any possible higher purpose for management? It's made up of people whose job is to oversee output. Front line management oversees individual contributors, the people doing the actual work of the organization. Moving up the hierarchy, middle management exclusively manages other managers—and hold progressively larger budgets the higher up they are. And executives are responsible for whole divisions or sections, including their people, budget, and physical assets. Taken together, management is the group of people invested with the authority to direct all of the activity and all of the assets at the organization's disposal. What could management possibly do that would be more appropriate or more useful than making sure the entire organization is always taking the next most reasonable step toward its goals?

Iteration requires feedback, and management is the system that provides it. It's the only system that can.

So what does management need to be doing so that it functions as the feedback system? In other words, how does management ensure that the organization Iterates? Clearly, this is critical information for anyone who manages other members of management, for anyone who advises them, and really for anyone with the word "*manager*" in his or her title. And while the answer isn't terribly complicated or hard to grasp, it's not particularly well understood, either.

That answer comes in the form of the Five Key Practices (and eighteen Core Components) of Iterative Management, and it starts in chapter 2. But before we dive in, we need to make sure we all know exactly what we're talking about when we use the word "management."

———————————  ACTIVITY  ———————————

Reflect on how management in your organization, including you, serves (or doesn't serve) as the feedback system.

1. To what extent do you as a manager clearly define one or more targets or outcomes for the people you manage as a group, analogous to the temperature setting on a thermostat?

2. How do you as a manager continually check and adjust the resources under your control to achieve the outcome(s)?

3. To what extent does your organization have one or more clearly defined targets or outcomes at the higher level?

4. How does the management above you continually check and adjust resources to achieve the desired outcome(s)?

## Misunderstandings about Management and Feedback

Management as we're discussing it here is often confused with managing and also with *change management*. In reality, each activity is different, and each involves its own type of feedback.

Managing is largely about enabling the people who work for you to succeed. It involves setting expectations, giving performance coaching, modeling and enforcing workplace standards, incentivizing and motivating people, delivering compensation messages, and supporting professional development. In this context, "giving feedback" means telling individual employees how they're performing, what they're good at, and what they need to improve. Managing well, and giving this kind of feedback effectively, is important for anyone with direct reports at any level. It should not be ignored.

*Change management* is primarily for helping large groups to acclimate to and implement major changes in things like direction, organization, or scope. It involves finding executive sponsors, planning communication timing and delivery, dealing with early and late adopters, and understanding the emotional and psychological impacts of major change. In this context, "providing feedback" means letting sponsors, executives, and other interested parties know how a change campaign is progressing. *Change management*, and giving this kind of feedback accurately, is important for anyone who needs to shepherd a large group of people through a substantial shift. It should not be neglected in those situations.

This book is not about managing, and it's not about *change management*. It's exclusively about management—a system of managers, operating in concert, constantly adjusting resources based on new information coming in to keep the business on target. Management involves defining and adjusting group output requirements, monitoring prognoses to hit future targets, coordinating complex efforts, enabling group work, and constantly asking the question, "What's the next most intelligent step *from here*?" Only in this context is it sensible to say that management is the *feedback system* of the organization. It's like the thermostat, keeping output on track despite fluctuations in the environment.

Just as Inuit Eskimos have fifty words to differentiate kinds of "snow," and ancient Greeks had six words to distinguish forms of "love," we could really use another word for "manage*ment*!" It would be nice to have a unique term for the concept of a set of individuals, vested with the resources of the organization, acting in a synchronized fashion to constantly ensure that the organization hits its targets.

If we had one, we might notice how little has been written about the topic—about what it means to be in manage*ment* and what it means to run a manage*ment* team—especially compared with how much has been written for other uses of the word. An overwhelming amount of advice for manag*ing* people has been produced, and a large body of work exists regarding *change management*. There's even guidance available on the topic of manag*ing* people who are manag*ing* other people. But for all that content, you'll find very little about manage*ment* as described here—how *you* should behave as a member of manage*ment* and how you should encourage and require the members of manage*ment* who work for you to perform this essential function, so that together you enable your part of the organization to Iterate.

This is especially unfortunate because, although manage*ment* doesn't take the place of manag*ing* or of *change management*, when done well, it does make both of them easier. By creating a context in which goals make sense, targets are aligned, and people are held accountable to reasonable, appropriate expectations, management makes manag*ing* easier. And by making the organization more flexible and adaptable, it renders the labor-intensive practice of *change management* necessary only for the most substantial changes.

Incidentally, good management is also supportive of good *leadership*. Exactly how that works depends on the definition you choose of leadership—we haven't been able to collectively agree on that one, either. But one of the few things nearly all our dissimilar definitions have in common is that leadership involves getting groups of people to do significant things—and no matter how you look at it, that requires manage*ment*.

We need to talk more about manage*ment*; this book is a guide to the topic for anyone who runs a management team or advises someone who does. It defines what manage*ment* is, describes in detail how it's supposed to work, and helps you determine what you can do to ensure that the manage*ment* that reports to you functions as a fast, flexible, focused team—rather than as a collection of disparate individuals manag*ing* a larger collection of even more disparate individuals.

As you read it, don't let mana*ging* or *change management*, with their other important kinds of feedback, distract you from the importance of *management acting as the feedback system of the organization.* If you and the managers who work for you aren't playing that part, then there's a gap in your organization that those other tools simply can't fill.

## ACTIVITY

First, reflect for a moment on the kinds of advice you can expect to take from this book.

1. As a manager, you can use it to inform the way you manage your own people and run your own team.

2. As a manager of other managers, you can use it to inform your expectations for those people, too—how you want them to behave with their own teams.

3. If you're in talent management, human resources, organizational development, or a similar role, you can use it to inform the guidance you give to those who manage other managers.

4. Since you also *have* a manager, you *could* also use it to guide your behavior with your peers and boss and to make suggestions to help improve that group.

Second, take a moment to reflect on the differences between the items on the list above. In particular—

- If you're going to do item 2, you had better also do item 1. If you really want the people on your team to behave in a certain way, there's no better approach than modeling it yourself.

- If you're going to do item 3 and you manage people in your own position, you had better also do item 1. The consistency between your behavior and your advice is a form of integrity. Plus, your personal experiences will make you a better teacher and adviser.

- No matter what you do, remember that you're always free to *skip* item 4. You don't *have* to get your boss to run his or her organization the way you want to run yours. In fact, pushing too hard will likely cause problems. It's perfectly acceptable to be liberal in making improvements in your own team or organization yet conservative in making suggestions to others.

Finally, before you read on, decide which of the numbered items above will be your focus for this book. Is there anything else not listed above?

# CHAPTER 2

# FIVE KEY MANAGEMENT PRACTICES

Information is a source of learning. But unless it is organized, processed, and available to the right people in a format for decision-making, it is a burden, not a benefit.
–WILLIAM POLLARD

Over the next five chapters, we'll be delving into a system of Five Key Management Practices. I summarize them with this graphic, in which each orange dot represents one practice.

We'll fill in labels for the dots as we go along, one Key Practice per chapter, starting in chapter 3. But first, take a look at the structure of the graphic. The reason for the circulation between the two large arrows should be obvious enough: Iteration means taking a step, learning from it, and then taking the next step—over and over again. But notice also that there's a path between any one orange dot and each of the others. That's a reminder that the practices are interdependent: they support and enable each other. Any one of the Five Key Practices alone may sound like a good idea, but if the other practices aren't also in place, it won't be nearly as effective as it could be, and real Iteration won't happen.

The Five Key Practices are known to be in place in the highest-performing organizations across a variety of industries—companies that, because they Iterate, are more efficient, effective, and flexible. As a result, they tend to beat their competition and perform very well in their market spaces. If you want to run a fast, flexible, focused management team yourself, the Five Key Practices (and the Core Components of each) are the best method gleaned from the last seventy years of work in sociology, psychology, organizational design, organizational behavior, and neuroscience.

Of course, since you're reading this book, it's likely that your organization is already reasonably successful. Managers in flailing, struggling organizations tend to focus less on topics like Iterative Management and more on tactical survival tools. Most likely, the organization you run is already doing at least some parts of the Five Key Practices. You're already, at some level, Iterating—even if you feel like you have a long way to go. So don't be surprised if some of this feels like "old news." If that happens, you may have uncovered one of your organizational strengths.

By the same token, don't be surprised if some of the Five Key Practices seem completely new for your organization or if you recognize their absence immediately. You'll probably spot some weaknesses, too. After all, if your organization were perfect, and if you were running it perfectly, you wouldn't need this book at all.

Realistically, life is seldom black and white. You and your organization probably aren't perfectly good *or* perfectly bad at any of the practices. Remember the three-part sequence—*understand, assess,* and *improve.* Focus first on understanding the behaviors the Five Key Practices describe and how those behaviors interrelate. Your assessment and your improvement plans will come as we go along.

Remember, too, that we're talking about behavioral practices, not abstract ideas. In presenting these concepts, I've found that this level of specificity causes language to become a challenge. The Five Key Practices are behaviors that have been discovered and validated empirically in successful organizations—*things people are actually doing.* But no matter *what I decide to call those behaviors,* any label I give them will necessarily be taken from terminology usually reserved for abstract concepts. So it's easy to get lost in the gap between the *things people are actually doing* and *what I decide to call those behaviors*—particularly if I happen to use words that already mean something specific to you or your organization.

We've already faced this problem once, in defining the word "management." It will happen again. In a later chapter, for example, I'm going to note that one of the Five Key Practices involves group decision-making. In this book, the term "Group Decision-Making" defines a specific set of behavioral practices: how a particular group acquires a certain type of information, processes it together, and creates a plan of action.

The thing is, you or your organization may already have your own definitions or ideas about *group decision-making*. The term may be included in your corporate values, in your operating manuals, or on posters in your hallways. Or perhaps you have done a lot of reading for yourself about *group decision-making*.

Either way, as soon as you read those three words in this book, we're at risk for a misunderstanding. You might assume your knowledge of *group decision-making* as a concept means that you're already practicing the concrete behaviors I'm describing. Or you might become curious to compare my philosophy of *group decision-making* with your understanding of the topic. Either way, if you allow yourself to become distracted by this accident of language, you'll probably fail to ask the only question that matters: whether the actual *behaviors* I'm describing are happening in your own organization—regardless of whether you and I would use the same *words* to describe them.

I don't have a perfect solution for this. There's no way to predict what each word will mean to each reader, and it's not reasonable to explore the possibilities for every term. I've seriously considered borrowing from another language to create the labels for the Five Key Practices. Such an approach was taken with lean manufacturing principles—you've likely heard of *kaizen* and *muda*, for example. But that creates the problem of constantly needing to translate. And I think having to keep a glossary in your left hand at all times runs counter to the goal of making things operate more smoothly.

So, my request is this: if I mention something that sounds familiar, obvious, or has a particular meaning in your organization, please stay open, stay engaged, and always assume that I am using the term differently than the way you've heard it used before.

It might not be true. It may turn out that what I'm talking about is exactly what you thought. As I've said, some components of Iterative Management are likely going on around you already. On the other hand, it just might turn out that I'm describing something that's unlike anything you're currently doing. The only solution is for you to withhold judgment until you're certain—to focus on the *behaviors* more than on the *words*.

---

## ACTIVITY

Reflect on the concept of Iteration as it applies to your organization.

1. If you had to identify one thing your organization does that helps it to Iterate—adjust intelligently each step of the way—what would that be?

2. If you had to identify one thing your organization does that hinders its ability to Iterate, what would that be?

## The Story of Alice

With that, we're ready to get specific. As an introduction to Iterative Management and an example of fast, flexible, focused management teams, let me introduce you to Alice. She works for someone named Max, and she has two peers: Bob and Cal.

---

### ▶ WATCH THE VIDEO!

Your copy of this book includes prepaid access to a library of videos, including *The Story of Alice.* You can watch the video now, then return to it later to refresh your memory or share concepts with others. Create your free account and watch any video, anytime, at **IterateNow.com**.

---

A regular organization chart for Alice would look like this.

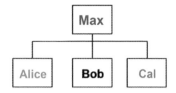

Traditional organization chart for Max, Alice, Bob, and Cal.

But Alice's organization purposely uses a different representation because they want to illustrate how the four managers work as a team led by Max.

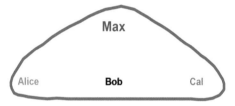

Max, Alice, Bob, and Cal as a team.

Alice is clear with herself and everyone else about what she's trying to deliver. In fact, she has abstracted her output into a short list of items that covers most of her work. She has three at the moment, though sometimes she might have as many as seven.

Each of those three things is a tangible, measurable, understandable output. For example, "Bring product A to market on schedule and under budget" or "Produce output completions to meet plan, which ramps up to 55 per week by year end."

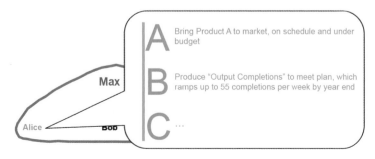

Alice's output list.

Alice frequently talks about her outputs. She has an elevator pitch—a kind of infomercial—in which she goes over the whole list in about ninety seconds. Whenever she introduces herself or begins a presentation, she starts with her list. As a result, everyone knows exactly what Alice is trying to do— they've heard her talk about it often—and they tend not to bother her with unrelated topics. She also has a single graph for each item on her list, all on a single page or screen. Every time Max holds a staff meeting, Alice puts it up so that everyone can quickly see how things are going for her.

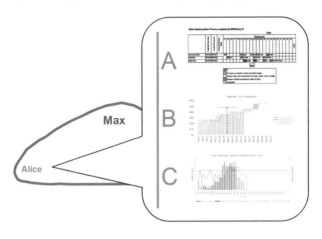

Alice's graphs.

Bob and Cal also have their own lists of outputs, their own elevator pitches, and their own page or screen of graphs. And since everyone on the team knows how to read everyone else's graphs, Max can get an overview of the work of his whole team in only a few minutes in front of everyone.

Max is quite specific about these graphical displays. He requires that they show whether *expectations for the future* have changed. This future focus is key not only to how his staff reports to him but also to how he runs his regular meeting with them.

As an example, let's take a closer look at one of Alice's graphs—the one where she's supposed to produce output completions to meet an increasing ramp plan. Until today, she's been on track for this particular output. Take a look: most of the blue bars indicating her past production are at or ahead of the plan represented by the solid orange line.

Produce "Output Completions" to meet plan, which ramps up to 55 completions per week by year end

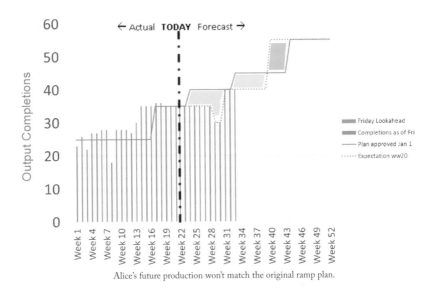

Alice's future production won't match the original ramp plan.

Now notice the forward-looking part of her graph. The orange bars and dotted blue line show that Alice expects to fall short of the plan during a couple of future time periods (shaded in yellow) and then to produce ahead of the plan later in the year (shaded in orange). This is the important part! Max and his team can't do anything about the past, but they can look at and respond to *changes in what's expected to happen in the future*—what's called "future variance."

Alice is definitely showing future variance. This might be something the rest of Max's team needs to know about, so she will get on the agenda for Max's next staff meeting. When it's her turn, she'll bring up her variance in a specific way:

- First, she'll remind everyone of her objective, the **output** she's trying to accomplish. This won't take long, as they've heard it before.

- Then, she'll show her **status** and how her expectations of the future have changed. Again, since they're familiar with her graph, this won't take long to explain.

- After that, she'll summarize the **issue**, the underlying cause of her expected variance. In this case, her resources are coming online differently than she'd expected, leading to delays in her ability to increase output relative to the original plan. She'll tell them this clearly and concisely.

- Finally, she'll make a **recommendation**, suggesting what she thinks should be done. In this case, she claims she can't prevent her output from falling behind in the first two time periods, but she thinks she can make up the shortage during the third time period—the one when she expects to produce ahead of plan—which will allow her to recover her overall targets for the year. To make that happen, she's asking Max and the team to reallocate some of Cal's money to her budget.

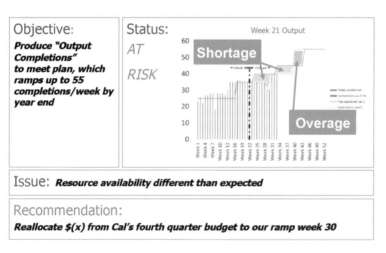

Alice's report to Max's team about her future variance.

When Alice is done with her presentation, which won't take more than about three minutes, Max will ask everyone at the meeting to *teach* him what they know about the situation. Cal will probably have something to say, since Alice is asking for his money! Bob might also have some ideas. Once Max is satisfied that he's learned what they know, he'll make a decision. Then the four of them will make sure they all have the same understanding, both about *what* Max decided and about *why* he decided it. Alice, Bob, and Cal will need that information when they take the decision back to their own teams.

Whether they like Max's decision or not, Alice, Bob, and Cal *will* take it back to their teams. They have a commitment to each other to execute group decisions, even when they don't personally agree. That way, if a decision is a good one, it will work. If it's a bad one, it won't work, and they'll know it. Either of those outcomes is OK with them, because either is informative, providing a clear next step. What they don't want is to have a decision fail and not know why—not know whether it failed because it was a bad decision or because personal agendas and sabotage prevented it from being implemented properly.

They certainly don't always agree. Alice, Bob, and Cal are only human; their opinions and their goals are often at odds. Actually, Max encourages them to share those disagreements during the decision-making process. As part of his learning, he wants to fully understand the reasons for them before he decides. "But remember," he tells them, "you can't bake one slice of a pie without the others. The definition of success for all of you is the same—it's whether or not, together, we achieve *my* plan. *We succeed or fail together.*"

Remember how Alice, Bob, and Cal each have a short, abstracted list of their outputs and an infomercial about them? Max has one too. At that level, Max's plan is Orange/Black/Green. That's why they represent his staff grouped together instead of in separate boxes—because he runs his staff *as a team*, the Orange/Black/Green team. Max's team exists to achieve the leader's plan, and they all know it.

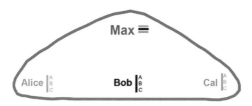

Max, Alice, Bob, and Cal with their output plans.

So if Alice and Cal disagree over whether she should get his money, that's fine. But they'll be arguing and advising Max about what's best for *Max's plan*, not what's best for each of their agendas. They may well have a heated debate over whether it would be better for Max's Orange/Black/Green plan to reassign Green funds to Orange or leave them where they are. What they *won't* have is a fight between Alice and Cal that sounds like "Orange ABC versus Green ABC." Everyone knows he or she is there to achieve the same plan—Max's plan. It's nonsensical to think that some pieces of that plan could "win" at the expense of other pieces.

In the end, whatever Max decides, the whole team will do. And in the process of the debating and the doing, Alice, Bob, and Cal will learn more and more about each other's work, too. That knowledge will make them even better advisers to Max next time. And it will especially come in handy if any of them is ever promoted to Max's job.

Meanwhile, Alice, Bob, and Cal do the best they can at their own jobs. They manage their teams in the same way Max manages them: Alice runs her Orange ABC team as a *team* aimed at completing Orange ABC, rather than as a collection of individual managers tasked *separately* with Orange A, Orange B, and Orange C. Bob and Cal run their teams the same way.

Lower in the structure, the front line managers reporting to Alice and her peers manage their individual contributors in a specific way too. They're careful to ensure that their employees have clear output goals, tools to track and adjust their own progress, and control of the resources they need to get the work done. This equips those individual contributors to work as efficiently as possible. More importantly, it enables them to give accurate forecasts to their supervisors—forecasts that make their way *up* the management chain, ending up summarized in graphs like the one Alice presented to Max and her peers, asking for budget previously assigned to Cal. Here's how it looks:

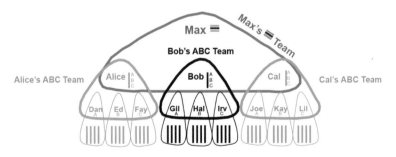

Max's entire organization, represented as Linked Teams.

Whatever Max decides about Alice's recommendation will get implemented as needed by the whole organization, flowing down from Alice, Bob, and Cal to the front line. And if that decision has any impact on output, within a week or two it will start showing up in new forward-looking forecasts—first from the front line and then from the management teams. Then those forecasts, appearing as graphs, will be used by the managers to make the *next* round of decisions and take the *next* round of actions.

That's how everyone in this organization takes a step, learns from it, and then takes the best next step. That's how they Iterate.

The Story of Alice may sound like somewhere you've worked, it may sound aspirational, or it may sound impossibly idealistic. But management teams truly can be this fast, flexible, and focused. Although decidedly different from the standard North American Management Model, a substantial number of organizations do work this way. They do Iterate. As a result, they're usually the highest performers in their market spaces.

---

## "YES, BUT NOT HERE"

As you read "The Story of Alice," you may be tempted to say, "This all sounds good, but it would never work in *my* organization." You may even find yourself listing practices, people, and other "realities" that seem to make Iterative Management impossible—and you may be disheartened by the notion that your culture "would never allow it."

Don't give up—especially not this soon! It's natural to feel uncertain, but don't let healthy skepticism turn into debilitating cynicism.

At no point in this book will you be asked to change the world—only to do things you can reasonably do. You'll always be starting with exactly one manager—yourself (or the person you're advising if you're in HR). There will always be *someone else* who won't agree to work Iteratively, whether a more senior manager, a board member, a peer, or a customer. Run your part of the organization as best you can, and deal with the other parts as you must. Simple, beneficial, local change is the only way culture change ever happens—at any level.

Remind yourself too that one can argue against literally any improvement by pointing to other people who won't agree—even in advance of fully defining what they won't agree to! Don't let "them" prevent *you* from fully *understanding* the Five Key Practices and eighteen Core Components of

Iterative Management, *assessing* how your current organization works and what benefit it could gain, and then finding small, feasible ways to *improve* it.

You'll find more information about defining first steps, changing culture by starting small, and facing down "the temptation to surrender" in chapter 8. Until then, focus on understanding what's here and experimenting safely where you can. Nothing in business ever happens until someone decides to make it happen, and understanding what's possible is always the first step.

---

If you're wondering how to run *your* organization to behave more like Max's, you're on the right track. We'll spend the rest of this book answering that question, using Alice's world as an idealized (if simplified) example of Iterative Management. Along the way, we'll investigate each of the Five Key Practices, defining it, breaking it down into specific Core Components, and looking at how Alice and the managers around, above, and below her use it. You'll be asked to reflect on the part of the organization you run, to think about how your management team compares to Alice and her peers, and to try some new behaviors yourself as you go along. By the time we're done, you'll *understand* how management enables an organization to Iterate, you'll be ready to *assess* your own organization's strengths and weaknesses, and you'll be positioned to help *improve* Iteration in your organization—with the management team you run (or advise) and any managers who report into it.

*Understand*, *assess*, and *improve*. That's our plan, and we're ready to begin.

## ASSESS FIRST

In a hurry to get a snapshot of your organization? Your copy of this book includes one prepaid license to take the "Assessment of Iterative Management Practices." Your instant, customized report describes how effectively both you and your manager use the Five Key Practices, and it helps you identify potential improvements. Create your free account and access your assessment at **IterateNow.com**.

## ACTIVITY

Think about The Story of Alice and about the ways it parallels your own organization (or doesn't).

1. In what ways is your organization most like Alice's? In what ways is it least like Alice's? In what ways is your approach to management similar to, or different from, Max's?

2. Draw yourself, your boss, your peers, and your reports in the "Linked Teams" format, as in the figure on page 22. Try filling in another layer or two below your reports if you can.

3. Circle yourself and any managers who report directly to you. These are your "primary targets"—the individuals whose behavior you may want to coach or adjust as a result of reading this book. Please realize that first on that list is you.

OR

4. If you're in talent management, human resources, organizational development, or a similar role, circle the leaders and managers whom you primarily plan to advise based on what you learn here. Remember to put yourself at the top of that list if you manage others.

# CHAPTER 3

# OUTPUT & STATUS BROADCASTING

You've got to be very careful if you don't know where you are going,
because you might not get there.
–YOGI BERRA

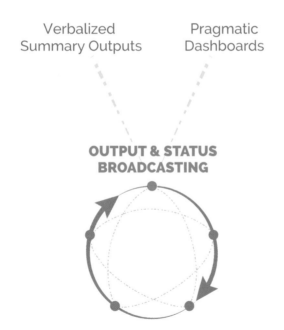

Verbalized
Summary Outputs

Pragmatic
Dashboards

OUTPUT & STATUS
BROADCASTING

It's an observation that sounds ridiculous: research indicates that good managers know what they're doing.

You're probably wondering, how obvious can you get? And who was dumb enough to pay for that research? Surely any such study would have ended with a request for a refund, if not worse.

But as I said before, if I say something that sounds obvious, please assume I mean something completely new and different. This is a good chance to practice.

We begin by investigating the first of the Five Key Management Practices: **Output & Status Broadcasting**. This practice has two Core Components, both ways in which managers stay crystal clear about what they're doing: they do so verbally via **Verbalized Summary Outputs** (the VSO) and graphically through **Pragmatic Dashboards**.

## Verbalized Summary Outputs

We'll start with the VSO, which is all about managers talking about what they're doing.

If you've ever worked in the world of sales, you're probably familiar with "the elevator pitch." In the time it takes you to ride an elevator with someone—about ninety seconds—you should be able to give a quick and compelling statement of what you're selling. That way, when the doors open, the other person can decide whether to continue the conversation. But while the sales version has become quite popular over the years, most people don't know about the other version of the elevator pitch—the one used by managers to discuss their outputs in Iterative work environments. That's the VSO.

Your VSO is a statement of the output you're trying to deliver. It's usually expressed as a list of statements that summarize the work of your group into measurable, countable outputs. Of course, the specific items within different VSOs vary widely, but the basic idea is to have three to seven items that together account for roughly 80% of your work. The list should take you sixty to ninety seconds to say out loud.

Once you've written them, that's what you do: you say them out loud. Frequently. It's no accident that the *V* in VSO stands for "verbalized." When you introduce yourself in a meeting, you lead with your VSO. When you sit down at lunch with some friends and they ask what you're working on, you lead with your VSO. When you meet with clients and you have to tell them what's new, you lead with your VSO. You can change the items on your list whenever you want, and you can adapt them to different audiences, but you're always sharing them, always publicizing them, always advertising your output commitment.

Make no mistake: the VSO is your output commitment. In fact, each item on your list must pass the "Look, Ma!" test. That means each one is tangible enough that when you get it done, you can metaphorically show it to your mother. "Look, Ma! We released this product to market." "Look, Ma! We produced seven hundred widgets as planned." "Look, Ma! Our revenue is up 15%."

The "Look, Ma!" test helps avoid vague, unmeasurable outputs—especially in less tangible areas such as knowledge work and influencing others. It forces discipline around defining what is truly measurable. Phrases like "position ourselves for success," "learn about the competition," and "facilitate conversations" are replaced with *outputs* like "discover our customers' top three priorities," "deliver an analysis of our major competitors," and "create a regular monthly forum." If you don't have something to show your mother when you're done, it's not a countable output. And if it's not a countable output, it's not a commitment you can make to your boss or your organization.

Drafting your own VSO can be a bit tricky, but you can't ask the members of your management team to do what you're not willing to do yourself. So try it! Start by jotting down all of the outputs you're working, through your team, to produce. Don't worry about how many points are on your list. Simply put down everything that comes to mind, as long as it passes the "Look, Ma!" test.

▶ WATCH THE VIDEO!

Your copy of this book includes prepaid access to a library of videos, including *Creating Your VSO: Saying No without Saying No*. You can watch the video now, then return to it later to refresh your memory or share concepts with others. Create your free account and watch any video, anytime, at **IterateNow.com**.

If you're like most people, you wrote down a lot more than seven items, and that's not even counting the ones you forgot. But the VSO shouldn't have more than five to seven items, because the list needs to be long enough to be meaningful yet short enough to be memorable.

How do you reduce the list?

First, drop low-priority entries. Eliminate anything that isn't critical.

Second, remove anything that would qualify as administrative. Things like travel, meetings, and reports are all real work—they occupy your time as a member of management—but they're processes, not output commitments. They don't belong on your VSO.

Third, if you still have too many outputs, combine what's left.

Combining does *not* mean gluing two different ideas together by putting the word "and" in between them. It means abstracting to a higher level. For example, maybe one of your outputs is to complete designs for some lower-cost replacement parts; you have a small department working on that. Another is to renegotiate some bulk consumable pricing with a vendor; you have two team members who manage your company's supplier negotiators. A third is to streamline processes that use hourly contractors, something your newest staff member is doing with her team. You could incorporate all three of those things into a higher-level output—something like "meet X% cost-reduction target."

Getting your *level of abstraction* right is key to your VSO. If you get too granular—if you try to list all seventy-eight ways you're trying to cut costs—then your VSO isn't memorable or easy to share. But if you get too abstract—if all you say is "I cut costs"—then your VSO isn't meaningful and doesn't represent a real output commitment. You have to find the middle ground.

Take another look at your own list. If you have fewer than three entries on it, make them more granular and less abstract. If you have more than eight items, first eliminate the low-priority and administrative outputs, and then make whatever is left less granular and more abstract.

You now have a draft of your own VSO. Of course, it's not *really* a VSO because you haven't verbalized it to anyone yet. (Little of what you do in management can be done all alone.) Still, you've made a start.

Consider Alice. With guidance from Max, she has created a VSO too. In her case, it's three items. For reference, we call them Orange A, Orange B, and Orange C, but she wouldn't use those terms. When she delivers her actual VSO, it probably sounds something like this: "Hi, I'm Alice, and I'm the manager of Orange. My primary goals are, first, to bring Product A to market on schedule and under budget; second, to produce 'output completions' to meet plan, which ramps up to 55 completions per week by year end; and third . . ."

Of course, if you read the text above out loud, you'll find that it only takes about ten seconds. But in place of saying "bring Product A to market on schedule and under budget," Alice would say a few words about Product A and why it's important, a few words about what the schedule requires, and a few words about the timing and rationale for the budget. With three to seven items on her list, Alice will end up speaking for between sixty and ninety seconds quite easily.

That way, in less than two minutes she can summarize what she has committed to deliver to Max and, by extension, the rest of the organization. Alice is polite, and she's not aggressive, but she's also not shy about sharing her VSO. When you first meet her, she shares it. When she introduces herself before making a presentation, she states it. When she's having a staff meeting, she reiterates it. Alice talks about her responsibility for Orange A, B, and C so often that everybody knows what she's working on and what she's committed to do. In their minds, Alice and Orange go together.

This may seem a bit repetitive, but a lot of good comes from it: It discourages people from distracting her with requests unrelated to her primary output. It gives Alice's boss a clear view into what she's doing and frequent opportunities to adjust it. It gives her peers a clear understanding of what she's working on and how it may affect them. It paints a clear picture for her direct reports of what's important to her and, therefore, to them. And last but not least, it lets all of those people and many others hear Alice *make a commitment* regarding what she will accomplish with her part of the organization. Since the fastest way to build trust is to *make and then meet commitments*, when Alice delivers on one of her VSO outputs, she'll not only be delivering the work the organization needs but also be teaching her employees, peers, and manager that she's trustworthy.

It's also not as redundant as it sounds. For one thing, it's not as if Alice reads the same exact words off a note card every time. Although she is consistent in talking about her outputs of Orange A, B, and C, she tailors the conversation to each audience. And since environments change rapidly, what she has to say about her output today is usually a little different than what she said last week or last month, anyway.

Now you understand the seemingly ridiculous assertion that good managers know what they're doing. They literally know *exactly* what they're doing— the specific output they're trying to produce, with the help of whatever group they manage—at an appropriate level of abstraction. And they make sure that everybody around them knows it, too. They're clear, specific, and politely assertive in broadcasting exactly what they are committing their group to deliver.

That's what Alice does at her level. It's what Max does at his level. And now, it's what you can do at your level.

---

## VSO CONVERSATIONS

The whole idea of the VSO is to use it as broadly as possible—reiterating it frequently to your manager, peers, and direct reports and using it as an introduction to others in the organization you meet—to create greater understanding and alignment. Sharing it takes no more than ninety seconds. But what happens next?

That depends on who's on the other side of the conversation.

With your manager, you'll want to frame your VSO as a sort of strawman proposal: "Here's what I'm working on, boss. Do you see anything I should change?" Undoubtedly, a "yes" will lead to a longer conversation than a "no." But either way, sharing the VSO creates a chance for the two of you to stay aligned about your work and to make sure your manager knows what you're doing.

With direct reports, you can be less tentative and more prescriptive. "Here's what I'm trying to achieve," you might say. "Let's talk about the work you're doing with your people and any changes in it, in the context of supporting my output commitments." Again, this will at times become a long conversation, but it will often be a short one if nothing has changed. Either way, it's an opportunity to confirm alignment and to help *your* reports to give *their* reports some line of sight into how their work impacts the bigger picture. It's also a chance to start encouraging the people who work for you to create *their own* VSOs, as it gives them a chance to experience both the VSO format and the conversation it sparks.

But what about sharing your VSO with your peers and with those in the organization who don't know you or your work well? As those conversations begin, you don't know whether or not the two of you have anything substantial to talk about—whether shared understanding and alignment would even be useful. The best way to find out is to notice the response you get from the other person immediately after you give your VSO. There are only three possibilities.

The first is an *affiliative* response; it's by far the most pleasant. This usually comes across as encouragement and even excitement. Your conversation partner will tell you how important your work is and start to explain how it relates to what he or she is doing. In this case, you need only do what feels natural: continue the conversation. Learn what the other person is working on, and explore whether there are ways for the two of you to collaborate or align efforts between your groups.

The second possibility is a *combative* response; this is the least enjoyable. It usually sounds something like this: "Why in the world are you working on *that*? Don't you know it will disrupt what I'm doing in this other area?" This response is often delivered with subtle (or not-so-subtle) cues of frustration or anger. Stay calm! Although this conversation is less agreeable, it's no less useful: you've uncovered a conflict that the organization needs to resolve, and it's up to the two of you to sort it out. Continue interacting. Listen to the other person's outputs and concerns, and see if you can make any headway toward addressing—or at least *understanding*—the contradiction you've discovered.

The third possibility is the *neutral* response, and it's about as bland as it sounds. Your conversational partner will probably nod and smile politely but express no real interest. You'll get few if any follow-up questions, and his or her attention may drift to other topics. Again, don't take this personally; it's simply a signal that your output and the other person's output don't relate to each other at the moment. It doesn't mean they never will—you never know what the future holds. There's certainly no reason for you to be anything but polite and courteous. Still, after making a little small talk, feel free to bring the conversation to a close. In this case, you truly have nothing more to talk about.

## ACTIVITY

It's time for you to put the *V* in your own VSO: you need to verbalize it.

1. Make sure the list you constructed while reading this chapter incorporates the majority of the outputs of all of the people and resources under your control. Then, take your draft list to at least three different people (five would be better) and talk through it. Try to keep to the ninety-second time frame.

2. Experiment with different audiences. For those with whom you work closely, including your manager and direct reports, note their feedback and the content of the conversation that ensues. For second-level reports and beyond—those who roll up to you—notice whether they immediately recognize alignment between their work and yours. For peers and other coworkers, pay special attention to whether their response is affiliative, combative, or neutral (see the VSO Conversations sidebar), and respond accordingly.

3. Adjust and refine the list as you go. Make it specific but not *too* detailed. You'll know you're making progress when your VSO starts helping you, and everyone around you, to know what you're doing and what you're promising to accomplish.

Once you have some experience using your own VSO, it's time to begin encouraging the behavior among the members of your management team.

1. Start with one person at a time, using *your* VSO to spark a conversation about *their* output commitments (see the VSO Conversations sidebar). Try to help them develop summaries of "Look, Ma" outputs during those discussions.

2. You may also be able to work with your whole team in a group setting, to create and share their VSOs and to discuss plans for encouraging the practice with their own direct reports who are managers. Consider setting aside time with your team for this specific purpose.

## Pragmatic Dashboards

The VSO is the starting point for Output & Status Broadcasting, but it's not the whole story. In the second Core Component, you turn the verbal information of the VSO into graphic information to be shared with the team. We call these data displays **Pragmatic Dashboards**.

You probably already have dashboards in your organization, so the word may have meaning for you. But I'm going to ask you, again, to forget about that for the time being. Please realize that what I mean by Pragmatic Dashboards may be something completely different than your organization's use of the term.

What's a Pragmatic Dashboard? To answer that question, let's go back to Alice. Remember, her VSO contains only three outputs: Orange A, B, and C. Anyone who works with her hears about those things pretty frequently. You've also seen Alice's Pragmatic Dashboard, the single-screen or single-page summary Max requires as an overview of the status of her entire VSO in graphic form. She doesn't show her set of graphs to everyone she shares her VSO with, but she does use it in regular meetings with her boss and team. Here's what it looks like again:

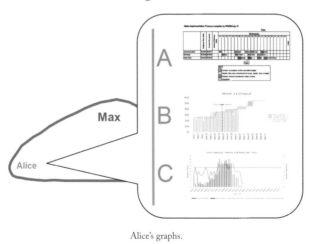

Alice's graphs.

Of course, every Pragmatic Dashboard is different. To make one, there are only two simple rules.

Rule number one: you get one graph per VSO item, and that's it. Remember the concept of *level of abstraction* when you were building your VSO? Keeping to one graph per item ensures that your level of abstraction is correct in your data displays as well as in your verbal summaries. It also means you won't be drowning your colleagues (or yourself) in unnecessary data.

Rule number two: those graphs must all contain what I call Really Useful Data. That's a term I made up. To understand it, let's start by looking at one of Alice's actual VSO items. Her Orange B item is to "produce output completions to meet plan, which ramps up to 55 completions per week by year end." (In real life "output completions" would be replaced with real units, like widgets built, services provided, or dollars collected, but this is specific enough for our purposes.)

Alice needs a single graph to illustrate this VSO item. The question is, what should it look like? Remember, Alice uses her graph with her boss, peers, and reports to describe *exactly* how her work is going. This allows interdependencies between her work and theirs to be discussed and equips the group to decide on the next most logical step from today. Put yourself in Max's shoes: what sort of graphical display of information can help him and his team to run that kind of Iterative organization?

Let's explore some possibilities and decide whether each one is good enough.

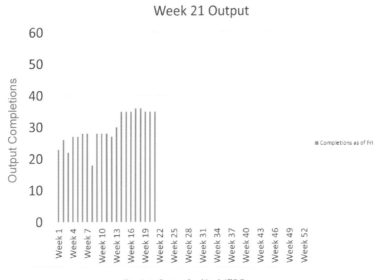

Graph 1: Option for Alice's "B" Output

In all of the options for Alice's "B" graphs, we'll assume that it's Monday of Week 21. In graph 1, Alice is showing total units completed weekly, from the beginning of the year until the end of last week, as blue bars. Do you think this graph will help Alice's group to Iterate? Is it good enough?

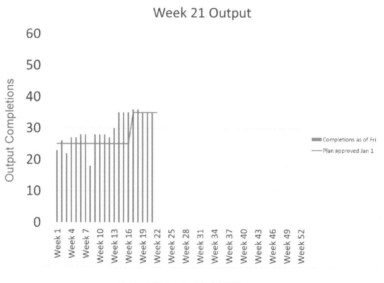

Graph 2: Option for Alice's "B" Output.

In graph 2, Alice has added the historical ramp plan as an orange line. You can see that, for the most part, her group has produced at or above the plan since the beginning of the year.

Do you think this graph is good enough?

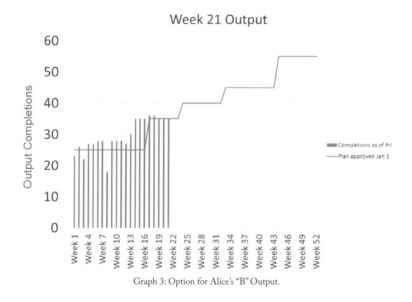

Graph 3: Option for Alice's "B" Output.

Graph 3 is the same as graph 2, except that Alice is now showing the ramp plan for the whole year. You can see that the orange line extends all the way to Week 52, and you can see where it reaches the goal of 55 units per week. What do you think about graph 3? Would it provide enough information for an Iterative discussion by Max's team?

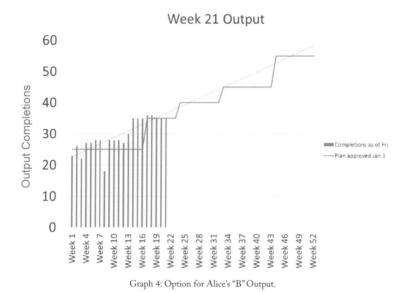

Graph 4: Option for Alice's "B" Output.

In graph 4 Alice has added a linear forecast line using the trend-line function in her spreadsheet software. If her output continues to meet the line, she'll be at or above plan for most of the rest of the year. What do you think of graph 4? Is it good enough?

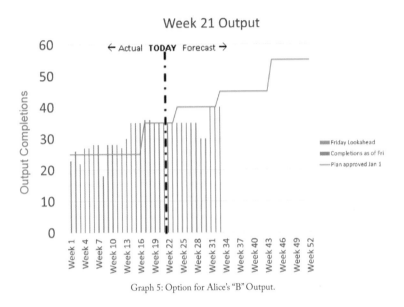

Graph 5: Option for Alice's "B" Output.

Graph 5 is a little different. The blue bars and orange line are still there, but Alice has dropped the spreadsheet forecast line and replaced it with a twelve-week look ahead that she conducts weekly with her group. The orange bars show what Alice and her group are forecasting to produce over the next twelve weeks. And it looks as though she's going to fall short of the ramp plan. What is your opinion of graph 5? Is it informative enough for an Iterative organization?

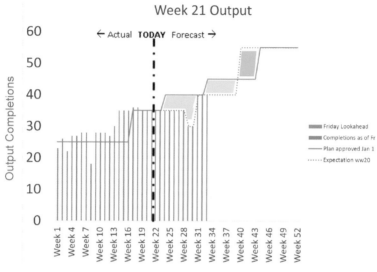

Graph 6: Option for Alice's "B" Output.

Finally, graph 6 is the same as graph 5, except that Alice has added a second forecast line. Every four to six weeks, she goes through this process, looking at changes in the availability of expected resources. As you can see, this line goes all the way to the end of the year, and she's shaded the places where it doesn't match the original plan. In the two yellow areas, she's expecting to fall short. And in the orange area, she anticipates exceeding the plan for a few weeks. Consider this last graph. Is it good enough to help Max's group Iterate?

I've found that when people evaluate this sequence of graphs, they grade more strictly as they go along. The first few graphs look pretty good when you have nothing to compare them to. But once you've seen graphs 5 and 6, you start wondering whether the earlier graphs are enough.

The truth is, those first few graphs are not enough—not if you want the organization to Iterate. Think back to the walk across the parking lot. When you're halfway to your car and you realize that you've been walking toward the wrong car, you change course. You don't do that by looking *backward* at the steps you've already taken but by looking *forward* at the difference between what you *previously expected to happen* and what you *now expect to happen*, given your current course. You say to yourself, "I previously expected this path to lead me to my car, but I now see that it is leading me toward a different car, so I need to make a change."

Really Useful Data doesn't only answer the question of how it's going. It also addresses the question of how the work is *going to go differently than you expected*. It contains backward-looking history, but it also contains *two* different versions of the future—an old one and a current one. You can call these whatever you like: old future versus new future, plan versus forecast, previous expectation versus current expectation. Whatever you call them, *Really Useful Data always includes the past and two futures*, and rule number two for making Pragmatic Dashboards is that every graph is built this way.

Graphs like 1, 2, and 3 are everywhere; they're typical of the North American Management Model. And they present serious problems for a group that is trying to Iterate. The group may be trying to take the next step based on a revised understanding of reality since the last step, but the information they need to do so is missing. Look again at those graphs; notice that none of them displays any insight about what Alice currently expects to happen. As a result, they can lead only to long-winded conversations filled with opinions about the future—"Oh, sure, I think we're on track"—without any data to back them up.

Graphs 5 and 6 definitely contain the two futures, so they pass the test. They're Really Useful Data. When Alice puts up one of these, the team can immediately see what she thinks is most likely to happen and what has changed, and they can consider what they need to do about the variance.

What about graph 4, the one that used the spreadsheet's trend-line function to create a forecast into the future? Is that a legitimate way to predict future outputs?

The answer is simple: it is legitimate only if it holds true. If Alice has reason to believe that her production in real life will actually follow the computer-generated trend line, then graph 4 is fine. But it's more likely that reality won't follow the simple algorithm, and Alice knows it. In that case graph 4 would be the worst one for Alice to use because it promises a future that she already recognizes as inaccurate.

Iterative organizations incorporate as much reality into decision-making and discussion as possible because the people in them understand that operating on inaccurate data is a direct path to failure. Nobody on Max's team—in fact, nobody in Max's organization—would ever intentionally bring an inaccurate forecast into a meeting. They wouldn't want people making real decisions and taking real actions based on unreal data!

As you've seen, Alice doesn't use graph 4 or any of the other faulty ones. She uses graph 6 with her boss, coworkers, and direct reports. She's very up-front about where she expects to vary from the original plan, quickly starting a productive conversation about whether anything should be done about the variance. That's what leads to a useful conversation regarding what to do about the future.

## DATA DISPLAY MATTERS

Do you go to a lot of bad meetings? Imagine sitting around a table with five other managers, having a meeting. What you're supposed to be doing is making decisions about how to manage the company into the future. Instead, one person talks for ten minutes about how well things are going in his group. The next person gives a ten-minute talk about how much travel she's been doing. A third person gives a ten-minute talk about upcoming absences and coverage plans. Maybe these speakers try to give opinions about what is going to happen in the future, or maybe they focus on updates about past results and current challenges. Either way, after an hour, each person has spoken for ten minutes and listened for fifty, yet no one is sure what to talk about. Besides, time is up, so the meeting adjourns.

That's a bad meeting. To have a better one, you need Really Useful Data: graphical summaries of measurable output that include historical data on past performance along with two futures—the old plan plus what you now expect to happen.

With that in hand, aimless monologues transform into specific discussions about the future: We can foresee a potential problem next month—how can we avoid it? What will we do during this upcoming shortage—will it cause any issues? And how about during this period of overproduction next quarter—will that cause any backlog for us or problems for our customers?

If each of the people in your imaginary meeting came in with one or two of these kinds of forward-looking graphs, the group could spend less than five minutes picking out the most important issue to talk about first and then spend the rest of the meeting addressing that issue and making some decisions. That's a good meeting!

But it's only possible with Really Useful Data.

## ▶ WATCH THE VIDEO!

To review this concept or share it with others, watch **Data Display Matters: Less Monologue Plus More Information Equals Better Meetings**—part of your free video collection included with this book. Create your free account and watch any video, anytime, at **IterateNow.com**.

---

## ──────── ACTIVITY ────────

Consider the data displays used in your organization.

1. Take a look at any important graph from your organization. Does it contain a history and two futures? Does it make it clear if there's a *variance*—a change in what you now expect versus what you previously expected?

2. To what extent do you use forward-looking graphs for your own output? To what extent do you encourage or require managers who work for you to do so with you?

3. To what extent is forward-looking data an important part of conversations with your boss and peers?

## Task Type Matters

I need to acknowledge an obvious but important fact: in the example graphs we just reviewed, we were looking at only *one* type of graph for *one* particular VSO item for *one* person. And you may be thinking that this sort of forward-looking data display works well for charting something like Alice's "output completions," but it would never be feasible for the work you or your managers do.

You're probably right.

Most of the graphs used on the management team you run will end up looking quite different from Alice's—in fact, Alice's own other graphs will be different from the one we've just reviewed. Alice's "B" Output example was useful in illustrating what we mean by Really Useful Data, but to start generating your own forward-looking graphs, you need more than a single example of a single graph of a single piece of output.

You need an understanding of Task Type.

What's Task Type? As it turns out, all workplace tasks fall into one of only three categories. Understanding these categories is critical because you can't even think about creating forward-looking Really Useful Data displays for any item in your VSO until you are clear about the type of task it involves.

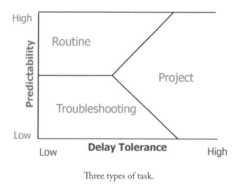

Three types of task.

The differences among the three Task Types are based on two simple characteristics of the task: *predictability,* which is whether the person doing the work can anticipate what it will be in advance, and *delay tolerance*, which is whether the task must be completed immediately or if it can wait.

When predictability is high and delay tolerance is low, we call this *routine* work. Examples include things like factory production and the processing of regular compliance paperwork for approval. The people doing this kind of work know what it will be before they start. They must maintain some sort of pace to keep the outputs on schedule, but the outputs themselves don't change much. Counting "Look, Ma" outputs of this type is usually no more involved than simply tallying the completion of each unit of output.

When foresight into the output goes away—when predictability becomes low and delay tolerance is low as well—we call it *troubleshooting* work. Technical support and disaster recovery are two examples of these tasks, which must be done quickly even though they're difficult to anticipate. Until a phone call or email comes in with a problem, the performers of troubleshooting tasks don't know what to expect; once the problem arrives, they need to move quickly to solve it. Quantifying this type of "Look, Ma" output generally involves some countable feature of the population of issues in queue—perhaps how many problems remain to be solved or how quickly they're being handled.

When delay tolerance moves from low to high—when people have more and more time to complete the work assigned—predictability becomes less important because there's more time to accommodate surprises and changes. This third category is what we call *project* work. Examples include construction projects and product releases. Project work has milestones and deliverables far in the future, and workers plan their tasks and manage themselves, at least to some extent, on the way to those outputs. The countable "Look, Ma" outputs here usually include both the final outcome and a set of subordinate outputs or deliverables critical to achieving it.

When it comes to Output & Status Broadcasting, Task Type is key for two reasons.

First, it's key to creating the VSO, because it provides a simple quality test regarding the level of abstraction of the items in it. Each of the three to seven items on the VSO must be composed entirely of one Task Type. If something is a blend of two or more Task Types, it's an indication that the author has tried to combine multiple different outputs into one item rather than abstracting the output to the next higher level.

Check your own VSO list now. If you find an item that appears to combine multiple Task Types, review the information about *level of abstraction* in the VSO section of this chapter. Edit the item so that it represents a single Task Type at a higher level, rather than a conglomeration of multiple pieces of subordinate output.

Second, Task Type is key to creating Pragmatic Dashboards, because it provides the starting point for creating Really Useful graphs. Even after you have an item of a single Task Type in your VSO, you still have to determine how to display it graphically as forward-looking Really Useful Data. Determination of the item's Task Type is the first step in doing so.

Appendix 1 of this book summarizes the three Task Types for easy reference, and appendices 2 through 4 contain information, examples, and guidance for charting each type of task. Read the one that corresponds to any

Task Type you're considering, and use it as a resource and starting point to create your own graphs.

## ACTIVITY

Scan appendices 2, 3, and 4 and look at the example graphs for each type of task. Consider which of these formats might make sense for displaying some of the outputs listed in your own VSO and some of the work delivered by the managers who report to you.

# SUMMARY: OUTPUT & STATUS BROADCASTING

*As we close out on each of the Key Practices, you'll find a summary and a final activity—a sort of rehearsal—to reflect on what you've learned and put it to use. Use them for yourself or as group activities and discussion items for teams of managers reading the book together.*

In Output & Status Broadcasting, Verbalized Summary Outputs help managers to be clear with themselves and each other about the output they're trying to deliver. Pragmatic Dashboards allow them to be specific about how they will deliver that output and about whether their expectations for the future have changed. All of this equips the management team with a solid understanding of what's going on and gives them a basis for asking the question, "What should we do *today* in response to what we've just learned regarding *tomorrow*?"

## ACTIVITY

Consider Output & Status Broadcasting in the context of your own part of your organization.

1. After you've tried your VSO on three to five other people and refined it as needed, choose one item on your draft VSO to represent as Really Useful Data.

   • Determine its Task Type. See appendix 1 for reference.

- Go to the appropriate appendix (2, 3, or 4) for the Task Type you selected. Review the sample graphs and choose one that would work for your own output, or choose one that could serve as a starting point for representing it.

- Create a graph of your output. If you have the necessary data and appropriate skills, you can work in Microsoft Excel or any other program, but that's not necessary. It's fine instead to draw your graph freehand, using only estimates of the information. You're not trying to create a final product here, just a concept sketch of what a good graph could look like.

2. Consider the graph you just created as you reflect on the following questions:

   - How does it represent past data—the history?

   - How does it represent two futures and any difference between your previous expectation of the future and your current expectation?

   - Which of your direct reports contributes most directly to the output measured in this graph?

   - In what meeting(s) would you present your graph and for what purpose(s)?

   - How do you think the other attendees there would respond if you were to present your graph? Would they be receptive? Combative? Something else?

3. Now shift your focus from your own output to the members of the management team you run.

   - Begin (or continue) encouraging your direct reports to create their own VSOs and share them with you. One way to start this conversation is to share yours and then say that you'd like to have a one-on-one discussion with each person to better understand how his or her output supports your own. You'll need to be extra careful to frame this as collaborative and not dictatorial. You're the boss, after all. Still, your reports will likely appreciate the one-on-one attention. In those conversations, help each employee work toward a VSO-type summary that both of you can remember. You may or may not want to teach the VSO acronym along the way.

- Pay special attention to the data displays and graphs your direct reports use. Do they align to the VSOs you're creating together? Do they display two versions of the future? Begin coaching your reports to include two sets of future expectations in their graphs rather than try to describe them in narrative form. Pay attention to whether this helps steer group conversations toward what should be done *today* to prepare for what's coming *tomorrow*.

# CHAPTER 4

# WORK PREVIEW MEETINGS

Light the path before you and you light the paths of those around you.
—REV. WALT BREWER

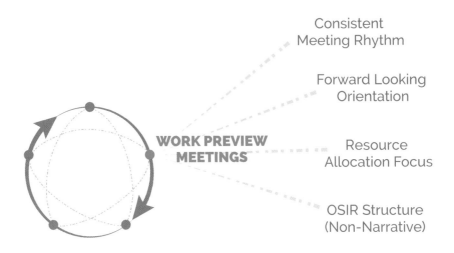

Consistent
Meeting Rhythm

Forward Looking
Orientation

**WORK PREVIEW
MEETINGS**

Resource
Allocation Focus

OSIR Structure
(Non-Narrative)

Now that we've finished discussing Output & Status Broadcasting, we're going to turn our attention to **Work PreView Meetings**. These meetings make use of the Really Useful Data we just discussed.

So far, I've referred to regular meetings, like Max's meeting with his team, as "staff meetings." But that's about to change. In an Iterative organization, Work PreView Meetings is the term we use for regular meetings between a manager and his or her direct reports. So Max has a Work PreView Meeting with Alice and her peers on a regular basis—probably every week or at least every two weeks. Alice has one with her team too. And so should you.

Work PreView Meetings can also be held by teams working on cross-functional initiatives, like task forces, project teams, and working groups—really any team whose charter is to allocate resources. Any management meeting can be a Work PreView Meeting. But since the structure and function of all Work PreView Meetings is basically the same, for now I'll simply use Max's meeting as an example.

By the way, this doesn't mean that you have to start *calling* your staff meeting a Work PreView Meeting. Remember, this book is about behaviors, not labels. Focus your attention on how we define the term and the extent to which similar behaviors are present now or could be adopted by you, your team, and your organization. If adoption of the *label* would help move the *behavior* in the right direction, go right ahead. If not, you don't need the distraction.

As with all the practices, we define Work PreView Meetings in terms of Core Components—observable elements that make it clear whether or not the practice is in place. In this case, we're looking for four of them: **Consistent Meeting Rhythm** and **Forward Looking Orientation**, which represent the *what* of the Work PreView Meeting; **Resource Allocation Focus**, which explains the *why*; and **OSIR Structure**, which defines the *how*.

## Consistent Meeting Rhythm

We begin in this section with the first part of the *what*: Consistent Meeting Rhythm.

Work PreView Meetings follow a consistent rhythm. They happen on a regular schedule. If Max is unavailable because he's traveling or with a customer, or if he goes on vacation (something we'd strongly encourage), the team doesn't cancel the meeting and delay all decisions until he returns. Max simply chooses someone from the team to take his position as the meeting leader. Alice, Bob, and Cal meet as usual, with one of them acting as the chair and decider until Max gets back. The same thing happens if Alice is going to be unavailable; she appoints Dan, Ed, or Fay to take her place in decision-making—both in *her meeting* and in *Max's meeting*. The meeting schedule doesn't get interrupted by the presence or absence of any one person. That's what I mean by *consistent*.

Depending on how things are in your organization, the idea of being consistent in this way may seem a little strange. After all, the boss is the one responsible for the team, right? If the boss isn't available, then what's the point of having the meeting? The boss isn't there to hear the updates, the boss isn't there to facilitate the discussions, the boss isn't there to make the decisions. Isn't the meeting without the boss an empty ceremony?

I've certainly seen situations where it was. Maybe you've seen this too: groups getting together without their manager because they were "supposed to." One common example is the mandatory staff meeting. The group talks aimlessly for an hour, sort of chuckling about why they bother to get together at all when the boss is out. Then they adjourn without having made even one useful decision. "We can't really do anything," goes the refrain, "because the person in charge isn't here."

Is the team useless if the person in charge is unavailable? That's the argument against being consistent. Before you decide, let's talk about the other aspect of consistent meeting rhythm: the word "rhythm."

We don't just say that the Work PreView Meetings in Iterative organizations are consistent; we say that they follow a consistent meeting *rhythm*. This implies a pulse, a steady and regular drumbeat, always in the background. In music the rhythm serves as the framework, the cadence by which everything else happens. The same is true in Iterative organizations. The rhythm of regular Work PreView Meetings serves as a backbone to the function of the organization, the cadence by which information gets moved, decisions get made, and instructions get transmitted. This cadence is critical in enabling your management team to Iterate.

How does this work? Maybe Max meets with his team every Tuesday and Alice meets with her team every Thursday. One Wednesday, two different members of Alice's team discover some problems with the ramp plan on her Orange output. So they bring the information up in Alice's regular meeting on Thursday, decide together to adjust their forecast, and do so. That change in expectations has implications for Max's team, so Alice presents it in his Tuesday meeting. She shares her newly adjusted forward-looking data with Max and her peers so they can decide what to do about it. Max makes that decision, and, whatever it is, Alice brings it back to Dan, Ed, and Fay in *their* next meeting on Thursday.

| Mon | Tue | Wed | Thurs | Fri |
|---|---|---|---|---|
| | **Max's** meeting | **!** Problem Discovered | **Alice's** meeting Forecast Adjusted | |
| | **Max's** meeting Change Presented Decision Made | | **Alice's** meeting Decision Communicated | |
| | **Max's** meeting | | **Alice's** meeting | |
| | **Max's** meeting | | **Alice's** meeting | |

Consistent meeting rhythm in Max's organization.

I'll cover the mechanics of those decisions and the meetings soon. For now, simply consider the benefit of the rhythm. Within about a week of discovering a problem that needed attention from Max, without anyone scheduling any special meetings, Alice's people are able to discuss the problem, define its impact, escalate to Max, get a clear decision back from his team, and discuss and implement that decision at their level.

More importantly, *everyone knows this is how the rhythm works,* even before anything comes up. When Dan and Fay individually discover problems on a Wednesday, they know Thursday is their chance to raise them with their boss and peers. In that meeting, Alice and her team know Tuesday will be Alice's chance to bring it to *her* boss, Max. And in *that* meeting, Max knows his decision will make its way back to Alice's team, for implementation, on Thursday. And this works, even if Alice is out—even if Max is out—because Max's meeting and Alice's meeting stay on the calendar even when they're not personally available.

That's the rhythm.

Now, imagine the alternative. Imagine that it's Wednesday and Alice's team has discovered a problem. But there's no Consistent Meeting Rhythm. Alice is out sick, and they've heard that Max is traveling internationally, so they're not sure if either meeting will happen. What do they do? Whom do they tell? Do they call a special meeting between themselves to make a plan? Do they keep quiet? Should someone escalate to Max directly? Does anyone dare escalate *above* Max if he can't be reached?

Without the rhythm, Alice's team is set up for failure. Maybe they keep quiet, or maybe they do a one-time escalation. Maybe they get lucky enough to figure out the right approach to keep themselves out of trouble and get the right information to the right people, or maybe they don't. Either way, by taking away the meeting rhythm, the company has burdened these people with figuring out *how to manage the organization* instead of with *actually managing it.* Every new issue presents a new problem to solve about what to do with the information. And every hour the team spends trying to figure out how to communicate the variance or the problem is an hour they can't spend addressing it.

Imagine if, while you were walking across the parking lot, your leg muscles needed a different amount of blood oxygen—a little more or a little less. But they had to stop and figure out the process of asking for it before they could make the request. *Every. Single. Time.* How much less efficient would the walk to your car be? You might never get there.

Is the team useless if the person in charge is unavailable? Only if the system makes the team useless. If there's a Consistent Meeting Rhythm, the team members can keep functioning. And that's a good thing, because someone is always unavailable. Someone is always out sick. Someone is always traveling.

If you don't have a Consistent Meeting Rhythm, your organization will have snags and stalls every time someone goes to the doctor or takes a day off. Coordinating work will become difficult. Iterating will be impossible. On the other hand, if you *do* have a Consistent Meeting Rhythm, your organization will keep moving information, keep making decisions, and keep carrying them out. Everyone who works for you will keep Iterating, even if someone gets the flu and you have to go overseas.

## ACTIVITY

As it turns out, a Consistent Meeting Rhythm—this regular cadence of decision-making meetings—is one of the most observable signs of an Iterative Management system. It's one of the easiest clues we have as to whether an organization is set up to Iterate. Reflect on the ways in which your own organization does—or doesn't—follow a Consistent Meeting Rhythm.

1. Consider the management meeting you run with your own direct reports.

   - Is the meeting held consistently, even when you or other members are absent?

   - To what extent do you communicate the notion that nothing should happen while you are away?

   - When you are going to be absent, do you appoint a delegate to act in your place?

   - To what extent do you authorize the delegate to make decisions and take actions on your behalf?

2. Do you encourage your direct reports in management to operate their own teams in this way? How could you increase this behavior?

3. Consider the management meeting that consists of you, your peers, and your manager.

   - Is the meeting held consistently, even when the leader or other members are absent?

   - To what extent does the leader suggest that nothing should happen while he or she is away?

   - Is a delegate assigned to take the place of the meeting leader when he or she is absent?

   - To what extent does the delegate have authority to make decisions and take actions on behalf of the regular meeting leader?

## Forward Looking Orientation

After Consistent Meeting Rhythm, the second Core Component of Work Pre-View Meetings—the other part of the *what*—is Forward Looking Orientation.

When I look at this whole body of work—all the Five Key Practices, all the Core Components—it's hard to imagine any of them seeming more obvious than Forward Looking Orientation. When a group of people are in the middle of trying to do something together and they meet to talk about it, they need to talk more about *what they're going to do next* than about *what they already did*.

We all know this, right? When you're walking across the parking lot, you look where you're going, not where you've been. Looking forward is intuitive. Looking forward is informative. Looking backward is, well, uninformative at best and dangerous at worst. I don't know about you, but I don't much care for the idea of walking backward across a busy parking lot.

Not only is Forward Looking Orientation conceptually obvious, but we've also already put it into practice. Remember the Really Useful Data we discussed earlier? It's distinctly focused on the future—on two futures, actually, and the difference between them. Really Useful Data is the basis for Work PreView Meetings, and it's always about the answer to this familiar question: "How's it going to go differently than we expected?"

Alice and her peers have already done the work of making their graphs look forward. Now Max, or whoever is leading in his place, is careful to facilitate a meeting that does the same thing: it focuses on the future and on what should be done *next* in service of the group's output goals.

That is easy to say, but it's not always easy to do. The two biggest killers of Forward Looking Orientation in management meetings are when meetings become overwhelmed by *discussions of status* and overwhelmed by *discussions of history*. You may have noticed your own meetings, or possibly lower-level meetings in your organization, getting sidetracked in this way. And the tricky part is that you can't eliminate either of these completely. Both are necessary, but both need to be carefully managed by anyone running a good Work Pre-View Meeting, including Max.

How does Max avoid these pitfalls?

Let's start with *discussions of status*. Since Alice, Bob, and Cal already have Pragmatic Dashboards, Max can open his meeting by having each person put up those visual summaries. This is simply a slightly modified version of the Verbalized Summary Output statement—the VSO. Take Alice, for example. Instead of stating her outputs—Orange A, B, and C—as she would in her VSO, she'll display her graphs. And since everybody's graphs are already familiar to everyone else, it doesn't take more than a minute or two for each person to give an overview. Alice might say, "Look, you know what I'm working on and how I measure it. As you can see, I'm OK with A. And I'm on track with C. But please focus your attention here: I have a serious variance on B. We'll be talking about that soon, because Max put it on our agenda for discussion, right after our updates."

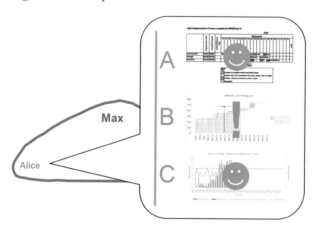

Alice's overview of her status and graphs.

This allows for a short discussion of status, but it also keeps the conversation moving. That's key. Because the truth is, as soon as someone spends more than a couple of minutes talking about how it's going in his or her area, everyone but the manager stops listening, and the time is wasted.

A little discussion of status goes a long way.

You might be wondering, why not skip the discussions of status entirely? Why not have Max go right into the problems at the start of the meeting? Why not start with the presentation of Alice's variance? It's tempting because they would save a few more minutes per person and get right into the heart of what needs discussing.

The problem is, if Max did that, over time the trust level in the group would suffer. Remember, the presentation of the VSO is the chance to make, and then meet, an output commitment. And trust is built by making and meeting commitments. Let's look at it from the perspective of Cal, one of Alice's peers. If the only time he ever hears from Alice is when she's got a variance or a problem, he will start thinking she's just a collection of problems—that she's not very good at her job. There's no context for her requests, no promise of useful output or history of delivering it. All she ever does is ask for help.

Of course, if that were how Max ran his meeting, Cal would only be making presentations that asked for help too. But Cal's perception of himself is different, because he can see everything he's doing. He can see that he's producing results—he knows that he's competent, that he's running his own area well, and that *his* help requests are only a small percentage of his work.

Everyone has that context for themselves; they need it for each other. Max needs his team to show each other that their work is ongoing and the house isn't on fire. He needs them to say, "I'm managing my area pretty well, and you know what I'm doing. I just need the group's attention and support *here*, on this issue, because it might affect our higher-level goals."

The short overview of the Pragmatic Dashboard encourages team members to respect, trust, and value each other. At the same time, it minimizes discussions of status. Max and his team can keep the process short and move on to the important issues of the day. Forward Looking Orientation means that discussions of status are *minimized* but not *eliminated*.

What about *discussions of history*, the second killer of Forward Looking Orientation? Like discussions of status, sometimes they're worth having.

For one thing, discussions of history can help the group decide what to do next. Maybe in the last meeting, Bob planned to interview some of Cal's employees about an ongoing issue. There's certainly nothing wrong with Cal asking Bob if he was able to get what he needed from them. That's a question about what's been done—about history—and the answer helps the group plan next steps.

Another way looking backward can be useful is to help define a current situation. If Alice's forecasts suggest the team will miss a commitment to a key customer, Max may want to consider the history with that customer. Have commitments been missed in the past? Have contractual or verbal promises been made? What has the customer said in conversations about competitors? This historical information may be critical as the group decides what to do now, *today*, about the variance they're facing.

Finally, groups can apply past experience to today's issues. Maybe Alice had a similar variance at about this time last year. Maybe Max had one several years ago when he was in Alice's role. Or maybe Bob had a whole other sort of problem last month, but in solving it the group came up with a headcount-sharing process that might help here. In all of these cases and many others, it's useful to discuss history and how it might apply to the situation now.

Like discussions of status, discussions of history shouldn't be avoided completely. But like discussions of status, they must be minimized, never allowed to become the main focus.

Forward Looking Orientation is that simple. When you minimize discussions of status and discussions of history, all you're left with are discussions about the future.

At its most basic level, the agenda for a Work PreView Meeting is "What's going to happen in the future, and what should we do about it now?" These meetings are all about defining and taking the next most logical step in the Iteration. Forward Looking Orientation means yesterday and today take a back seat to tomorrow because tomorrow is the only thing the management team can truly influence—and that's as true for your team as it is for Max's.

---

## ACTIVITY

Reflect on the Forward Looking Orientation of your own organization.

1. Consider the management meeting you lead with your direct reports.

   - To what extent is the meeting forward looking, as opposed to backward looking or history focused?

   - Approximately what percentage of time in each meeting is spent discussing status, discussing history, and discussing the future? Do you think any adjustments in this balance would be beneficial?

2. To what extent do you encourage your direct reports to manage their own teams in this way? How could you increase this behavior?

3. Consider the management meeting that consists of you, your peers, and your manager.

   - To what extent is the meeting forward looking, as opposed to backward looking or history focused?

   - Approximately what percentage of time in each meeting is spent discussing status, discussing history, and discussing the future? Do you think any adjustments in this balance would be beneficial?

## Resource Allocation Focus

Now you know *what* a Work PreView Meeting is: a meeting that happens regularly and always looks to the future. This brings us to the third Core Component—Resource Allocation Focus.

Resource Allocation Focus is *why* we have Work PreView Meetings. It's the reason for the Consistent Meeting Rhythm and the Forward Looking Orientation: the only way any manager at any level can adjust the next step an organization takes is by adjusting the *allocation of the resources under his or her control*. In Work PreView Meetings, managers decide how to allocate resources based on a new understanding of the future.

In many organizations, a lot of activity other than making resource allocation decisions goes on in management meetings. Employees like Alice find themselves fielding questions from Max about how certain initiatives are progressing or trying to explain why they made certain decisions. Managers like Max find themselves trying to create clear guidelines for things like absentee policy or fielding questions about senior executives' philosophy. And all attendees find themselves sitting through long-winded narrative presentations designed to explain how things are going in others' areas.

I don't mean to suggest that all of that is wasteful, though I have no doubt that some of it is. Some of it may be a necessary part of manag*ing* the individuals in the organization. Some of it may be useful for other reasons. But none of it is part of manage*ment*—the topic of this book—or what, specifically, the management team needs to be doing to enable the organization to Iterate.

Remember, *management is the feedback system*. It has only one purpose: to monitor the organization's output and make adjustments accordingly, so that the system continues to take the next most reasonable step given the newest information available. And none of the "other" activities above will contribute much to the process of Iteration.

Resource Allocation Focus—assigning resources differently—will.

Think of it this way: When you're in the middle of the parking lot, having just taken a step toward your car, and you want to get there as efficiently as possible, what matters most? Obviously, it's taking the next step. And that step is executed as the cumulative effect of a series of decisions that shape it. Decisions like which muscles get triggered, which ones get relaxed, how blood flow changes, and so on. All of those are resource allocation decisions, and they're the only decisions that matter for Iteration. If they're not made, or if they're not made correctly and in coordination with each other, the system fails to Iterate.

The same is true in management. Whatever the topic of discussion is in any given moment, the ultimate goal in a Work PreView Meeting is to make a decision about what to do with the resources at hand: given what we know now, and given what we have to work with, what should we do?

Obviously, specific resources vary. They could be budget dollars, equipment, or people. In a high-level executive team, they might involve thousands of people and millions of dollars. Lower in the organization, resources might be limited to only a few employees and a few pieces of equipment. But at every level of management, the Iterative question is the same: what, if anything, should we do differently with our resources based on new information?

"Differently" is a key word, because another thing that's the same at every level of management is that *all of the resources are already allocated*. Budgets are written, equipment is running or idle, people have assignments. There are truly only two options when it comes to resource allocation: resources can either be left alone or they can be moved around (*reallocated*). That's the only decision to be made, and it's the one that gets made, over and over again, in the Work PreView Meetings of Iterative organizations.

That's exactly what Max's team is going to talk about when they review Alice's graph. They will have just learned that her production is going to fall short of plan during two time periods and exceed plan during a third one. They need to decide whether there's anything the organization should *do differently* in light of that new information—and if so, what that is. Their answer can only come in the form of a resource allocation decision.

## MANAGEMENT IS ALWAYS RESOURCE CONSTRAINED

One of the unfortunate truths of management is that managers often find themselves resource constrained, stuck making difficult decisions about what *not* to do. *Not* funding important projects, *not* hiring much-needed staff, and *not* purchasing useful equipment are painful choices, yet being forced to say "no" in situations like these is often an indication that things are going *well*.

How can that be?

Consider management's critically important job: to assign resources to accomplish work. In an ideal world, the pairing would be perfect. Management would have exactly the resources it needs to accomplish a clear and complete list of necessary outputs, and its only task would be to map one to the other.

That alone might be challenging enough, but unfortunately, the real world is even messier. The amount of resources available *never* matches the potential workload. This is partly due to fluctuations in the availability of resources but mostly due to the infinite nature of work itself. There's always *another* product that could be developed, *another* customer that could be pursued, *another* improvement that could be deployed. There's always something else that *could* be done.

All of those possible outputs aren't created equal. Some products and services generate higher margins, some improvements generate more benefits, and some development projects carry less risk. And some of that potential work might be downright wasteful! So management isn't only tasked with figuring out what work *could* be done; it's also required to sort out which of all the possibilities would be most valuable.

All of this leads to a limited number of possible scenarios:

If management has *more* resources than valuable work to do, that's a problem—and not a good one. It means the company is wasting time, money, and equipment on low-value output. Resourcing worthless output is a path to bureaucracy and collapse.

If management has *fewer* resources than high-value work to do, managers can try to do *everything*. But there are limits to how many initiatives a person can accomplish, how far a dollar can stretch, and how widely a piece of equipment can be shared—and spreading resources too thin is another form of waste. It's much better to succeed at one or two tasks than to fail at ten.

The only remaining option, then, is the best among difficult scenarios: having fewer resources available than potential high-value work to apply them to and then intentionally *not* doing some of that work. By identifying the highest of the high-value outputs and then resourcing those fully and *at the expense of the others*, management is in the best possible position.

That's the unfortunate truth for you and all the managers who work for you: difficult though it may be, the best-case scenario is to be constantly leaving high-value work on the table because it's *a little less* high value than the work being done. It's always better to have too many options than too few.

---

## ACTIVITY

1. Consider the management meeting you lead with your direct reports.

   - To what extent is the meeting focused on making decisions about the *reallocation* of resources based on new information?

   - What other topics are major focuses of the meeting? Do they distract from or complement the Resource Allocation Focus?

2. How can you help your direct reports focus their management efforts more on resource allocation?

3. Consider the management meeting that consists of you, your peers, and your manager.

   - To what extent is the meeting focused on making decisions about the *reallocation* of resources based on new information?

   - What other topics are major focuses of the meeting? Do they distract from or complement the Resource Allocation Focus?

## OSIR Structure

Alice has discovered a future variance in her output: she expects different results than her production targets at three points in the future. And she needs to alert her peers and boss because it may impact their work and because she might need their help. So what's the best way for her to get Max's whole group focused on making the appropriate resource allocation decision?

To answer that question, we need to turn our attention away from the *what* and the *why* behind Work PreView Meetings and move on to the *how*. Work PreView meetings function well because the presentation of issues within them follows a specific structure—what we call an OSIR Structure, which is essentially the opposite of a narrative structure.

OSIR is an acronym for four things—the *only* four things that are needed for one manager to make a report to another about future variance in a staff meeting and set up a useful conversation about it.

**O**bjective
Planned measurable result

**S**tatus
Prognosis/likelihood, and variance

**I**ssue
Root cause of the variance

**R**ecommendation
Suggested action (help and/or adjustment)

Elements of an OSIR Report.

### OBJECTIVE

The *O* stands for objective, which is simply the output the presenter intends to deliver. Often, this is an item that comes straight out of the VSO.

When it's Alice's turn on Max's agenda, she'll start with her objective: to produce output completions to meet plan, which ramps up to 55 completions per week by year end. This is already one of the items on Alice's VSO—so, like you, the members of Alice's team have heard it before. In the OSIR

Report, this serves as a quick reminder to set the context for what's to come, and it takes only a few seconds.

## STATUS

The *S* stands for status. This is the prognosis, or how the future is looking relative to the original objective. Of course, if things are going as expected— if the prognosis is good and no variance is expected—there would be no OSIR Report to make. So this section always contains some version of a difference between two futures, as in, "Here's what I *used to* think would happen in the future, here's what I *now* think will happen in the future, and here's how they're *different*."

We've already investigated how to display this kind of information efficiently by using Really Useful Data. So it should be no surprise that Alice presents her status by displaying her forward-looking graph. Again, like you, Alice's teammates have seen the graph before, and they know how to read it. That's why it takes only a few seconds for her to direct their attention to the important areas and to what has changed.

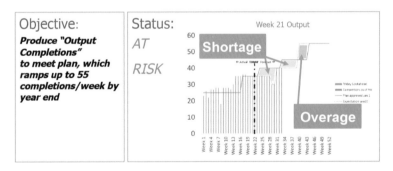

Alice's objective and status.

Note that in addition to showing the graph, Alice adds the phrase "at risk" to clarify her status. As with everything else in this book, that label itself isn't important, but the concept behind it is. The OSIR process works best with only three possible status categories, which might be named with colors, emoticons, or labels:

- Green, "on track," or ☺ means there's no change, and therefore there would be no discussion. This label would appear in a Pragmatic Dashboard but rarely in an OSIR Report since none would be needed.

- Yellow, "at risk," or ☺ means there's some variance and that it could possibly be corrected, maybe with help from the group.

- Red, "behind," or ☹ means there's such a large variance that the original plan will probably not be recovered and those impacted will likely have to adjust to the change.

Three status categories for OSIR Reports.

If your organization already uses these colors, emoticons, and labels in other ways, you could always invent new ones. It doesn't matter what the categories are called. What's important is that the definitions are consistently used to express the difference between the old future, or what we *thought* was going to happen, and the new future, or what we *now think* is going to happen.

That's all the information needed under status, and it doesn't take long for Alice to explain hers.

## ISSUE

The *I* stands for issue, and this is simply the reason for the variance. It's not a long-winded narrative discussion about who is at fault or a catalog of excuses for what happened. Rather, this is a short list of one item—or at most, two—explaining the root cause of the change in expectations.

Alice has probably been talking for less than a minute when she's ready to move to her issue. Here's what she tells the team: resource availability is different than expected, and that's what's causing the projected shortfalls and overages in the graph.

Of course, in a real-life OSIR, Alice would be more specific—it's people, equipment, funding, or something else that is becoming available on a different timeline than she originally expected,—and she would quantify the resource and the change as much as she could.

For the purposes of our example, her simplified statement will suffice. We, along with Max's team, now understand something about what's driving her variance.


## RECOMMENDATION

Finally, the R stands for recommendation. This is the longest part of what is ultimately a very short presentation. It answers one simple question: what does the speaker suggest that the group do about the variance?

Broadly speaking, there really are only two possibilities here:

- The speaker can make a help request. This is typically used for "yellow" or "at risk" items in which the owner of the output is telling the group, "If you could help me in the following specific way, I could recover and return to the original plan—or at least get close to it."

- The speaker can instead suggest that, colloquially speaking, the group should "get used to it"—adjust to the new forecast. This is typically used for "red" or "behind" items in which the owner of the output is advising the group that the variance can't be recovered and that they should therefore adjust their own work accordingly.

Of course, whether the speaker is asking for help or suggesting the group adjust, either way the recommendation is one of resource allocation. Because that's all a management group can do.

In Alice's case, her recommendation is something of a blend of these options. She is primarily making a help request: she suggests that the group reallocate a specific amount of funds from Cal's fourth quarter budget to her ramp in week 30. This, she believes, will allow her to pull in the overage that's she's now expecting in week 40 backward to week 35. She wants to do this—to start the orange overage in her graph *sooner*—because she believes it will enable her to reach her total output target for the year.

She's also highlighting the fact that this approach will still involve two periods of underproduction and a single period of overproduction between now and year end: the yellow sections won't go away, and the orange section will go on for longer. So there *is* an aspect of "get used to it" in her recommendation as well. The team will need to adjust to a different ramp than originally anticipated.

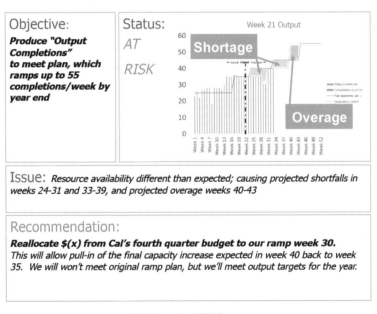

Alice's complete OSIR Report.

Alice's whole OSIR Report takes about three minutes, possibly less. In that short time, she reminds the group of her output commitment, she clearly states her prognosis, she lets them know what's driving the variance from her original plan, and she makes a clear, complete, actionable recommendation that—if adopted—would reasonably address her issue. That's how Alice quickly sets the group up with a possible action, and then she stops *presenting* and opens up the meeting for a *discussion* about her proposal.

▶ **WATCH THE VIDEO!**

Your copy of this book includes prepaid access to a library of videos, including *The OSIR Report: Create Useful Action in Staff Meetings*. You can watch the video now, then return to it later to refresh your memory or share concepts with others. Create your free account and watch any video, anytime, at **IterateNow.com**.

When she's done, Max and his team will have to have that discussion, and they'll need to make a decision about Alice's recommendation. In the next chapter, we'll take a detailed look at how they do that.

But for the moment, notice the advantages of both Output & Status Broadcasting and Work PreView Meetings in getting Max's team to this point: thanks to clarity on everyone's part about Alice's intended output, thanks to good habits around data display, and thanks to shared discipline around holding regular, future-focused, resource allocation meetings, the whole management team is equipped to have a productive discussion about what they can do *now* in response to *new information about the future*. This is management behaving as the feedback system. This is the core of Iteration.

## GETTING INFORMATION
## WITHOUT CAUSING TROUBLE

The OSIR Report is the linchpin of the Work PreView Meeting. It holds everything together. It's the best way we know for someone to create useful action in a meeting. Compared to a narrative status update, it's shorter, it's more targeted, and it sets the stage for group problem-solving rather than forcing everyone to listen quietly while one person talks.

You may be wondering, though, whether it needs to be so structured. If we don't want Alice going on and on about all her work, that's fine. But if shorter is better, why can't she just come in with a simple question? "Hey, Cal, I'm running behind on my Orange B output; can I have some of your budget to fix it?"

The thing is, sometimes—especially in sensitive, difficult, or emotional situations—the mere act of *asking* a question can provoke a defensive, combative, or otherwise problematic response.

Why? Because for all their utility, questions are verbally aggressive.

First, the asking of a question forces its recipient into a specific topic of conversation, even if it's an uncomfortable one. Second, the asking of a question suggests that the asker is *owed* an answer, which implies a status difference. Third, the asking of three or more questions in a row is a way of dominating a conversation by controlling the flow of information.

That's why, in sensitive situations, it's often much better to use an alternative information-seeking strategy—something other than a question.

One such alternative is the straw man proposal. In this approach, you state your own understanding tentatively, then invite edits to it: "Here's what I understood; please correct me as you see fit." This puts both parties on the same side of the metaphorical table.

Another alternative is to simply state your agenda without asking a question: "I wanted to share something with you about the work I'm doing and the problems I'm having. That's why I'm here." This allows the other person more conversational options.

Finally, you can use this formula: "When you $X$, I interpret $Y$," with $X$ as a behavior and $Y$ as an interpretation. This might sound like: "When you don't turn in your report, I interpret that the data aren't available"—or "that you don't think it's important" or "that you don't care about me." This creates a clearer separation between objective events and subjective beliefs.

Of course, whichever strategy you use, remember that intentions matter most. If you're judging, evaluating, or criticizing, the other person will know it, and you'll come off as disingenuous. On the other hand, if your intent honestly is to seek information, these strategies are often more effective.

That's why Alice is better off making an OSIR Report than bluntly asking Cal for his resources. First, her objective and status provide a clear statement of her agenda and explain what's not going as she expected. Then, her issue and recommendation create a straw man proposal for the group to consider. Finally—and equally importantly—when she stops talking entirely, it opens the meeting up for discussion. The OSIR Structure ensures that Alice doesn't force the topic of conversation, doesn't put Cal on the spot for an answer, and doesn't imply that her work is somehow more important than his. And while none of that guarantees the conversation in Max's meeting will go smoothly, it does increase the chances that it will.

▶ WATCH THE VIDEO!

Your copy of this book includes prepaid access to a library of videos, including **Get Information without Causing Trouble**. You can watch the video now, then return to it later to refresh your memory or share concepts with others. Create your free account and watch any video, anytime, at **IterateNow.com**.

--- ACTIVITY ---

Reflect on the use of OSIR Reports in your own organization. (Ignore the OSIR label and focus on the behavior.)

1. Consider the extent to which you require your direct reports to use an OSIR Structure when discussing issues in your own staff meeting. To what extent do presentations:

   - Start with a brief statement of an already well-understood objective (objective)?

   - Present a clear indication of future variance from an established plan (status)?

   - Indicate the most likely root cause of the variance (issue)?

   - Make a well-formed recommendation that is appropriate for discussion and action by the group (recommendation)?

   - Accomplish all of the above in about three minutes, so that the bulk of group time is focused on discussion of decisions and actions rather than presentations?

2. What could you do to improve your own management meetings in this area?

3. OSIR Reports aren't always appropriate for individual contributors, but they *are* used by managers at all levels. If some of

your direct reports manage other managers, what insight do you have into whether their staff meetings use an OSIR-type structure rather than a narrative structure? One clue may be the types of updates they bring to your meeting.

4. What could you do to encourage improvements in your direct reports' staff meetings?

5. Consider the extent to which you and your peers use an OSIR-type structure when discussing issues in your supervisor's staff meeting (and other meetings). Specifically, to what extent do presentations:

- Start with a brief statement of an already well-understood objective (objective)?

- Present a clear indication of future variance from an established plan (status)?

- Indicate the most likely root cause of the variance (issue)?

- Make a well-formed recommendation that is appropriate for discussion and action by the group (recommendation)?

- Accomplish all of the above in about three minutes, so that the bulk of group time is focused on discussion of decisions and actions rather than presentations?

## SUMMARY: WORK PREVIEW MEETINGS

Work PreView Meetings are where managers go to raise issues and make decisions. The Consistent Meeting Rhythm ensures there is a forum to raise each issue. Forward Looking Orientation and Resource Allocation Focus ensure that each conversation is about what to do with resources in anticipation of what's to come. And the OSIR Structure helps frame the issue efficiently, leaving maximum time for productive discussion.

ACTIVITY

When we closed on the first Key Practice—Output & Status Broadcasting—you attempted to draw a freehand graph of at least one

of your most important outputs. Now, it's almost time for you to embed that graph in an OSIR Report of your own.

Before you start, remember: these practices are about behaviors, not labels. If the rest of your organization isn't familiar with the OSIR acronym, you should absolutely *not* try to teach it to them as part of your presentation. It's fine if you never even mention any part of the acronym and if you remove the *O*, *S*, *I*, and *R* labels from your materials. You absolutely don't want to get caught up in a debate about format.

Simply build a presentation that has the same four elements— objective, status, issue, and recommendation, preferably in that order—in three minutes or less. Then present it at an appropriate meeting and in an appropriate way to get the group talking about *taking action on your recommendation.*

You *do* want to get caught up in a debate about your output, if a debate is needed.

1. *For yourself:* Create an OSIR Report for a piece of your own work, based on the freehand graph you drew in the last section. Ideally, this is something you would present to your peers and manager in a staff meeting, either to ask them for help or to notify them of a change you expect due to a future variance. Try to select a real situation from your work that will be worth their time.

   - Write your objective, which should probably be an item from your VSO.

   - Define your status. At a minimum, use a categorical statement like "at risk" or "behind" and summarize the situation verbally. If possible, include the forward-looking graph you worked on in the previous chapter, or one like it.

   - Write a short statement of the key issue, or root cause of the variance.

   - Write a feasible, actionable recommendation for the group to consider.

   - If possible, present this to an appropriate forum in three minutes or less, with an emphasis on asking the group to take action on your recommendation. (Even if you won't be presenting it, create it. Doing so will help you clarify your thinking and give you some experience before you ask your direct reports to use the format with you.)

2. *For your team:* Make a plan to experiment with an OSIR-based meeting in your own staff meeting. How will you teach your direct reports the simplified OSIR format and encourage them to bring up their most important issues that way? How can you increase the amount of time spent on future-looking discussions?

  • Keep talking with your staff members about the forward-looking graphs they're creating and how important those can be to making good decisions. But don't make changes to your meeting until you read the next two chapters. For now, start thinking and planning for how your meeting might change if it were more focused on future-variance discussions driven by OSIR Reports.

3. *For your managers of managers*: If you manage people who manage *other managers*, meet with them directly to discuss the idea of the OSIR Report and non-narrative staff meetings. Talk with them about the relationship between forward-looking graphs and OSIR Reports for the managers they manage. Find out whether they perceive any need for improvement, and consider how you might encourage, support, and/or even directly drive improvements in *their* staff meetings.

CHAPTER 5

# GROUP DECISION-MAKING

Bullshit is a greater enemy of the truth than lies are.
–HARRY FRANKFURT

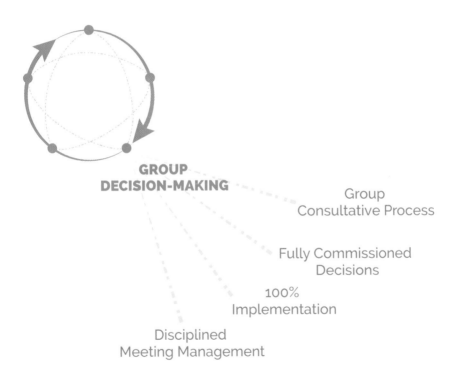

**GROUP DECISION-MAKING**

Group Consultative Process

Fully Commissioned Decisions

100% Implementation

Disciplined Meeting Management

Alice has completed her OSIR Report. She stated her objective, her current status, the issue causing the variance in her output, and her best recommendation of what Max's team should do. Now what?

Now Max must guide his team—Alice included—to use their Work Pre-View Meeting to make a decision in light of the new information. This will be a resource allocation decision representing the next most logical step, given all of the information they have now.

Here's where you start to see management serving as the feedback system for the organization, like a thermostat. Max's team has noticed a change in the metaphorical room temperature in the form of Alice's graph. Now they'll decide whether to turn something off, to turn something on, or to do nothing. It's by making decisions like this one, over and over again, that the organization Iterates.

But unlike the decision faced by the thermostat, this one involves more complexity and more options. Max's team could choose to follow Alice's recommendation exactly. They could decide to do nothing, signaling that they're not worried about Alice's variance at all. Or they could invent a third alternative, some option Alice didn't think of. Whatever they decide, their decision may have ramifications for other members of Max's organization, possibly both inside and outside of Alice's group. In real life, things get complicated fast, and Iterating isn't easy.

So how do groups of managers make decisions like this one?

The answer is, they decide as a group. And they do so in a specific way, by using the next of our Key Management Practices: **Group Decision-Making**.

Once again, we'll find four Core Components that together define the *what*, *why*, and *how* of the practice: a **Group Consultative Process**, which defines *what* the group does; **Fully Commissioned Decisions** and **100% Implementation**, which are *why* they do it; and **Disciplined Meeting Management**, which explains *how* they do it.

## PURPOSE AND MEMBERSHIP

Purpose and membership are the two most important definitions you make for any meeting.

Both are also automatic for direct-line management staff meetings. The purpose of Max's management team is *to allocate resources to achieve Max's output targets;* the membership of Alice, Bob, and Cal is dictated by the organizational structure. Those same definitions apply to any management team meeting in which the leader directly supervises the other managers in attendance, including yours. So you don't have to redefine purpose or membership when you gather the managers who work for you, because the answers are always the same. (Just make sure the attendees know what they are!)

You *do* have to define purpose and membership when creating other types of management meetings. The Key Practice of Group Decision-Making applies equally to all management meetings, but those meetings won't function well without a clearly defined purpose and the right membership involved.

Begin with purpose: clearly define *what the team is supposed to accomplish*. Generally speaking, there are two options for management teams. You can either charter a short-term *task force* to recommend solutions to a problem or organize a longer-term *working group* to make and implement decisions involving the allocation of shared or cross-functional resources.

Once your meeting's purpose is defined, it's critical to define the membership correctly—to get the right people, and *only* the right people, involved. Determining who they are will depend on the meeting's purpose.

A *task force* solves a problem. For this kind of meeting, you'll need one person from each pertinent area of expertise, and each will probably need to attend personally rather than sending a delegate. You may need to add experts as you further define the problem, but you'll also want to limit total membership to no more than nine individuals—five to seven is ideal. With too many people, effective interaction won't be possible, and the meeting will stall. So if your problem is so complex as to require ten or more experts, you'll need to split it into subordinate problems and coordinate multiple task forces.

A *working group,* on the other hand, allocates resources. For this kind of meeting, you'll need individuals with authority over each of the resources in question to attend consistently or send a delegate (in this case that's fine). You may also need others to represent demands on those resources; those people might or might not attend every time. Here attendance can get quite large. Just know that if your meeting includes more than nine people, you'll have to charter out subgroups to bring back recommendations on complex issues. A large working group's responsibility is to approve or decline recommendations, not to attempt to solve problems together in real time.

Whatever kind of meeting you're running, remember: if you don't have a clearly defined purpose and you don't have the right people around the table to achieve that purpose, all the Group Decision-Making discipline in the world won't help you get to a useful result.

## Group Consultative Process

Let's begin with the *what*—the Group Consultative Process.

When you run a group of people who need to come to a decision, it falls to you to determine *the process they'll use to decide*. And your decision about process must be made in advance, before the first decision about content is put before the team. This doesn't happen automatically—in fact, there are multiple possibilities.

One way to proceed is to agree that everybody's vote is equal and that there can be no change or action until everyone agrees completely. This is called *consensus* decision-making, and it does produce high-quality decisions. The problem is that it's extremely slow—so slow that it's almost never feasible in fast-paced business environments.

A modified, faster technique is called the *democratic* method. In this approach everyone still gets a vote, but there's no requirement that the vote be unanimous. If enough people approve a given change or action, the group goes forward even if remaining members oppose it. Conceptually, everyone's still treated as an equal; it's just that the group accepts some disagreement in exchange for the time savings. But voting presents two major problems. First, expertise gets weighted equally with everything else. If only one person understands the technical, market, or financial challenges involved with a decision, he or she can easily be outvoted. More importantly, this approach encourages people to spend their time gathering *support* instead of *information*. "I'll vote with you on this one if you'll vote with me on the other one" is a common phenomenon. Unfortunately, this and other kinds of politicking are a recipe for poor-quality group decisions.[2]

Of course, in groups like Max's (and yours), the people around the table are not simply a collection of equals. One of them is the boss! By organizing a group around one such person, called the "decider," additional decision-making alternatives become possible.

The simplest of these is to just have the decider *tell* everyone else what to do. This is called the *dictatorial* method. It's by far the fastest option, but then

---

2 Variations on the democratic method, such as requiring more than a 50% majority or assigning more weight to certain voters, are numerous. None, however, solves its fundamental flaw: voting encourages politicking and popularity contests in lieu of information exchange.

it's hardly a *group* decision. In this simplistic approach, the decider doesn't take into account *any* of the expertise of the team members. This is a dangerous way to make important resource allocation decisions in a situation where the subordinates are the ones who fully understand the challenges and dependencies.

There's an obvious fix. Rather than deciding unilaterally, the decider can talk to each member of the team and get his or her input before making a decision. This is commonly called a *consultative* model of decision-making. It's preferable to the dictatorial method because it involves more information, and it's preferable to the consensus method because it's faster. But this approach retains some of the same problems of the democratic method; team members simply turn their attention from trading votes with each other to *convincing the boss to go their way*. And there's another problem: the kinds of resource allocation decisions management makes are complex and multifaceted, and one-on-one conversations between boss and employee may not be enough. Often, only by hearing the proposals, challenges, and conversations of their peers can individuals give complete input to the person who is their manager and decider.

All of this leads to the need for a process in which everyone involved with the decision is talking with the leader and *with each other*, all at once. That's the basis for the *Group Consultative* approach: the decider attends a meeting in which he or she *learns* as much as possible and then *decides* as well as he or she can. In the meeting, members work to *teach*, not to convince; they teach what they know to each other and especially to the decider. And the decider's decision is not based on popularity or majority opinion; it's whatever the decider believes is best.

When it comes to Group Decision-Making for management teams, the Group Consultative Process is the best way to balance decision quality with time constraints. Consensus takes too long; the democratic approach gets sidelined by politicking; the dictatorial method suffers from both politicking and a total lack of information; and the basic consultative process encourages politicking and reduces information flow by isolating the conversations. Only the Group Consultative Process gets everyone talking together, in front of each other, about the impacts of various options. Only the Group Consultative Process puts content experts in the mode of *teaching* rather than *influencing* the decider. And only the Group Consultative Process endows the leader with the authority to make unpopular decisions only in light of *all* the information. The Group Consultative Process is the best option for the kinds of complicated resource allocation decisions management makes regularly so that the organization can Iterate.

That's the method Max uses in his Work PreView Meeting. After Alice finishes her OSIR Report, the whole team will have an open conversation to decide what they should do about it. Remember, we're talking here about behaviors, not labels. Max's group is going to have a real *conversation*, among all of them, about Alice's request for Cal's funds. They're *not* going to go around the table, one at a time, taking turns sharing their opinion in thirty seconds or less. They're *not* going to go away for a day and come back with seven-minute responses based on a PowerPoint template. They're *not* going to put it to a vote. And yet they're also *not* going to have an unstructured free-for-all in which the loudest, pushiest, meanest, or highest-ranking person wins. They're going to have a *real, functional conversation*—a useful group interaction in which they teach each other, especially Max, what they know about this situation. As it goes on, Max will do his best to understand everything his team is telling him. And when there's no more to understand, he will make his decision.

Please notice that although Max is trying to *understand*, he's not worrying about whether or not he *agrees*. There's a big difference! I might tell you, for example, that I want to buy the largest SUV I can afford. I think that in an accident, the safest place for my family to be is in a very large vehicle, and safety is my first priority. Now, you may think that a smaller vehicle can be equally safe if it's designed well or that I should focus more on fuel efficiency. But it's possible for you to *understand* my position without *agreeing* with it.

Separating the two—understanding versus agreeing—makes Max's life as manager and decider a lot easier. Whatever the content of the conversation, whether someone is teaching him about a fact, an opinion, or a desire, he can put his focus squarely on *understanding*: "I understand that your calculations indicate this action will cause sales to drop 10%." "I understand that you're strongly opposed to moving in this direction." "I understand that your life will get more complex if we implement this proposal." He can say those things and then follow them with, "Do I have that right? Is there anything else I need to know?" This discourages his team members from saying the same things over and over again. They quickly learn that once he understands them, that part of the conversation is over. By not offering his agreement as an option, Max keeps his team focused on information exchange instead of politics.

Still, you may be thinking that this whole process seems easier said than done, and if so, you're right. Rarely is any process easy if it involves humans with differing opinions. When issues get emotional and the stakes are high, every form of Group Decision-Making is challenging. And although groups can make better decisions than individuals, they can also make far worse ones. For the Group Consultative Process to stand a chance, "members teach and the decider learns" is only the beginning of the story. There are a few other elements that need to be in place as well.

First, and most obvious, once Max has made his decision, the whole group has to fully understand what it is, and why he decided the way he did, before they put it into action. We'll talk more about that next, with Fully Commissioned Decisions.

Second, a "group decision" is meaningless if people leave the meeting only to do whatever they want. Alice, Bob, and Cal must implement *all* of Max's decisions, even the ones they don't personally like. We'll also cover that later in this chapter, with 100% Implementation.

Finally, running a meeting like this requires a good meeting process and the right kinds of participation from the members. Otherwise, it will become a free-for-all. We'll go into details about that near the end of this chapter, with Disciplined Meeting Management.

The thing is, those *whys* and *hows* are secondary: they arise only because Max—and, I would argue, all of management in Iterative organizations—uses a Group Consultative Process for decision-making. The process may not be easy, but it is effective. Max uses it because he knows it's best for making complex, multifaceted resource allocation decisions. He takes decision-making seriously; the decisions he makes with his team can have ramifications across the whole organization and well into the future. And they come up all the time, over and over again, because the organization is Iterating.

▶ WATCH THE VIDEO!

Your copy of this book includes prepaid access to a library of videos, including *The Group Consultative Process: Group Decision-Making That Works*. You can watch the video now, then return to it later to refresh your memory or share concepts with others. Create your free account and watch any video, anytime, at **IterateNow.com**.

─────────── ACTIVITY ───────────

Consider the five types of Group Decision-Making: consensus, democratic, dictatorial, consultative, and group consultative.

1. Which one(s) do you most often use with your direct reports? Why?

2. Which one(s) do you think the managers who work for you use the most with their reports and teams? Why?

3. Which one(s) does your boss most often use with you and your peers? Why?

4. Which one(s) do you think are most common across your organization? Why?

5. Are any of them prohibited or frowned on in your organization? Which ones? Why?

## Fully Commissioned Decisions

*Why* does an Iterative organization practice Group Decision-Making? The answer has two related parts: first, groups like Max's team need to make Fully Commissioned Decisions, and second, they need to implement those decisions 100%.

Have you ever been in a group that had a discussion and then came to a decision, but only *sort of*? Perhaps you thought you knew what the decision was, but later you found out that someone else had a different idea? Or maybe you could tell in the meeting that one person wasn't on the same page? This is a pretty common problem. Too often we find out after the fact that a supposed group decision wasn't clearly or consistently understood by the group after all.

At best, this misalignment is a waste of the team's effort, forcing everyone back together to rehash everything. Often, it's worse: people don't usually recognize that they're not aligned until they act on their mismatched interpretations and their actions conflict. We're talking about management here— people who direct groups. By the time these conflicting actions are underway, whole sections of the organization can be well out of sync with each other. The costs in time, money, frustration, lost opportunity, and even employee engagement can be extreme.

That's why it's important to be clear: a group decision isn't a group decision until members of the group understand it *so well* that they continue understanding it long after the meeting is over and they're back in the confusing, conflicting reality of their real jobs. To make that happen, everyone in the group must understand both the decision itself, or *what* was decided, and the rationale behind it, or *why* it was decided. Otherwise, it's likely the team will end up misaligned.

In Max's meeting, once Alice has made her presentation, the group has had its interaction, and Max has made his decision, he will consider those same two components of the group decision. To ensure that he's made a Fully Commissioned Decision, Max will stop—literally stop the meeting for as long as necessary—to make sure that everyone understands *what* he decided and *why* he decided it. That's the decision and the rationale. Notice too that, again, we're talking about *understanding* and not *agreement*. Team members need to understand the decision and rationale, even if they don't agree with it.

The beauty of commissioning is that by staying focused on that two-part result—understanding the decision and the rationale—the process becomes exactly as simple or complicated as it needs to be.

Here's what I mean: Alice recommended that Max reallocate budget from Cal's group to hers. Imagine that after Alice had finished her OSIR Report, Cal had told everyone he had had a project cancellation in his group and he unexpectedly had a budget surplus. It wouldn't have taken much discussion after that for Max to be ready to give Alice what she requested. *Simple decisions with simple rationales are simple to commission.* In this case, Max's commissioning would have consisted of little more than stating his decision and rationale to the group—"I'm going to approve Alice's request since Cal has a surplus and her output is a priority"—and then asking if anyone had any questions.

Alice wasn't that lucky. A much more complex discussion ensued after her OSIR Report. While the group agreed it should be a priority to get Alice back on track, the majority of Cal's funds couldn't be reallocated, and no other budget was available. So after a lengthy discussion, Max decided that Cal would, in fact, transfer *some* funds to Alice but only a quarter of what she'd recommended (which was still more than Cal wanted to give). Max also decided that Bob would share some staff members with Alice at the point of her next production dip, to aid in her recovery. This represented a change in schedule for some of Bob's work, which would need to be communicated to customers. You know the story: often when you change one thing, a lot of other things change as well. Max's group is tasked with keeping track of all of the impacts, and they know it.

Outcome of group decision regarding Alice's OSIR Report: annotated slide.

*Complex decisions with complex rationales are complex to commission.* In this case, Max will need to spend more time talking with the team. He'll want to make sure they're all clear about the various parts of his decision itself, like exactly how many staff members Bob should share with Alice. And he'll also want to make sure all of their questions about his rationale are answered—including questions like "What's our message to the employees being reassigned to Alice about why their work for her is more important than the work they were already doing?"

Obviously, commissioning is an imperfect process. Since one person can't ever be sure of the contents of another person's mind, Max can't be certain that everyone understands his decision and rationale perfectly. It helps if he uses Disciplined Meeting Management—we'll come back to that later in this chapter. But however he does it, Max understands how important commissioning is and how it maximizes his chances of alignment.

There's also a simple test Max can use to see whether or not he's succeeded with commissioning; I call it the "alignment test." When he thinks everyone is in alignment, Max can stop and ask Alice, Bob, and Cal to take a minute or so to silently write down his decision and rationale, each in their own words. Then they can go around the group with each person reading their notes aloud and Max going last. If even one team member's understanding of Max's decision and rationale doesn't match his own, Max isn't done commissioning.

This can be an eye-opening process, and I'd encourage you to try it with your own decisions on your own teams. It's amazing how differently two people in the same room can interpret the same information, even when they're honestly doing their best to stay aligned. The sooner you uncover and address those differences, the better off you are, and the better off your team is, too.

In the end, whether the decision and rationale are simple or complex, the rule for the decider is the same: *you're not done deciding until you're done commissioning.* The decider who announces a decision and moves on without any discussion isn't enabling the team to act on the decision coherently and, therefore, isn't helping the organization to Iterate.

---------- ACTIVITY ----------

Consider the extent to which your organization produces Fully Commissioned Decisions.

1. How often and how completely do you commission your decisions in your own team meetings? How could you improve?

2. Try the "alignment test" with your team after you've made a decision, and note the result. How clear are your team members on your decision and rationale?

3. If you manage people who run their own management teams, how effective do you think they are at commissioning their decisions in those forums? How might you help them improve?

4. How often and how completely does your manager commission decisions with you and your peers? What questions could you ask after a decision is made to help improve alignment and shared understanding?

## 100% Implementation

Let's go back to your walk to the car. Perhaps you're halfway across the giant parking lot when you realize you've been headed toward the wrong vehicle. It's tempting to see that as either bad luck or bad planning. But the reality is that precisely *because* you've gone that far, you can now see that your car isn't where you thought it was.

The basic premise of Iteration—and the reason it works—is that with every step you take, you gain more information.

The blindingly obvious implication is that you have to, in fact, *take the steps* for this to work. Once you've decided on the best course of action, you can't get any smarter until you act. Iteration doesn't work if you simply stand in the doorway, considering your options and never taking a step into the parking lot. Iteration doesn't work if you take a half step, tentatively, and then back up, see if anything went wrong, and then take a half step in a different direction. Iteration requires definitive action. You have to choose a direction and start walking.

That's why the second *why* behind Group Decision-Making—what's arguably the real reason for it—is to create 100% Implementation of decisions. You need the organization to act on its decisions so that it can gain the information that only comes from having acted. That's the only way to Iterate.

The decision by Max's team concerning Alice's Orange B output had implications for Cal, Bob, Alice, and others, including Max. No doubt, it took some time and energy to reach that decision. So once it's decided and commissioned, it's critically important that the team members carry it out—that is, bring their resources into full compliance for 100% Implementation.

But what if it's a bad decision?

Winston Churchill said, "Success is not final; failure is not fatal." That's a great way to think about Iterating. Each decision along the way—each Iteration—may seem better or worse at the time, but the aggregate of all of them ultimately gets you where you're going.

## MANAGEMENT IS ABOUT BEING "WRONG"

After you get across the parking lot to your car, if you were to compare your actual path to a map of the shortest possible distance there from the door, you might become quite critical of your route. You might say to yourself, "I crossed this row of parked cars too far to the north, and I went around these traffic cones on the wrong side, and along this part of the path I was going in the wrong direction for several steps."

To judge this as wrong, of course, is to presume you had the map before you took the walk. If you'd had it, you would have used it! The whole purpose of Iteration is to find a reasonably efficient solution when you *don't* know the optimal one. What seem in retrospect like missteps were, at the time you took them, the most intelligent next steps you could find.

The same is true in management: nobody has a map! All you can do is gather as much information as reasonably possible and then make and implement a decision in a timely manner. Once you do, it's almost guaranteed that someone will appear with contrary information. Going after this market has brought challenges from a competitor; doing this reorganization has created undesirable attrition; handling this customer issue in this way has angered another customer.

*And you should have anticipated this!* Right?

Maybe. Management *is* responsible for practicing good Group Decision-Making. If you're not putting the right people in meetings to make decisions and if you aren't structuring those meetings to maximize their chances of making intelligent ones, then it might be true—maybe management "should have" foreseen certain issues.

On the other hand, anticipating every problem is impossible. People with contrary data may only come forward after implementation is underway. And that's not because those people are all negative, unhappy, dysfunctional critics. It's because the impact you're creating only becomes recognizable to them after the work has begun.

Action creates information. You can't discover you're walking toward the wrong car until you start walking. And your colleagues can't discover that your work is impacting theirs until you start working.

If you're in the business of management, you should get used to the idea that you're going to be wrong—a lot. Whatever seemed like the next most logical step yesterday will seem like it was a mistake in light of the new information you have today. And whatever you take as the next most logical step to fix that mistake today will probably seem like a mistake again in light of the information that surfaces tomorrow.

That's not a series of poor judgments. That's Iteration.

Despite the fact that Alice, Max, Bob, and Cal will make the best possible decision they can, given the facts available, it's entirely possible their decision won't end up producing the results they want. If it doesn't, they'll need to make another decision as soon as they realize the variance. Luckily, since every Work PreView Meeting is focused on variance, they'll notice soon.

On the other hand, the decision might work perfectly. In that case, there won't be anything else to talk about relative to Alice's Orange B outputs for a while, and they'll focus their meetings on other outputs and talk about other variances.

Either of these results is OK. Either is Iterative.

What's not OK is if the team fails to implement the decision 100%—for any reason.

Bob may be frustrated by Max's decision to move his people to Alice's work. What if he delays the transfer of personnel so that when Cal transfers the funding as agreed, there's nobody to use it? Alice may be annoyed that Max didn't transfer more of Cal's funds to her. What if she goes to Max behind Cal's back and convinces him to hand over even more of Cal's budget? In these and so many other scenarios, Iteration fails because the team can never learn from the decision. If things miraculously work out well, there's no shared understanding of why. More likely, things don't work out, and the team ends up in confusion—misaligned on what's going on and never having learned from the decision because of a failure in implementation.

And that's to say nothing of the damage to trust when people make commitments in the group meeting and then fail to meet them.

It's entirely possible Bob won't personally agree that it's a good idea to lend his employees to Alice, that Alice will think she should have gotten more of Cal's funds, or that Cal won't agree that sharing *any* of his budget is the best solution. Management can be a disagreeable business! During the consultative portion of the process, all of them are obligated to share those objections. Max has told them, "I expect you to share your disagreements. Do not keep them to yourself!" And he actively works to *understand* them. But all of that happens during the teach-and-learn discussion. Once Max's decision is made, Alice, Bob, and Cal don't have to agree, but they do have to implement.

Max's group, like all groups practicing this kind of decision-making, have an agreement with each other, a sort of contract, called *Disagree and Commit*. It's a commitment that Max requires from everyone who joins his team: to engage fully in each decision-making process and to commit fully to each decision that comes out of that process, even the ones they don't personally agree with.

Disagree and Commit contracts vary, but they always have three things in common. First, team members agree to *explain the rationale* when they communicate decisions to subordinates and others. When Bob tells his employees they're being loaned to Alice temporarily, he tells them why. And he does it using "we" not "they" language. He doesn't say, "Max and those people did it to us because *they think x, y,* and *z*." He says, "We decided this as a management team because *we think x, y,* and *z*." This reinforces to subordinates that the management team is functioning cohesively.

Second, as we've been discussing, team members agree to align their resources to every decision. That's 100% compliance every time. Once the team decides that Bob should give up two employees for six months, he does it, and he does it on schedule, even if he disagrees. That's the only way to ensure that the team benefits from the decision—that it becomes a step in the Iteration.

Finally, team members allow and encourage each other to seek contrary evidence, as long as they do so without sabotage. If Bob didn't agree with Max's decision personally, it would be disingenuous for him to pretend that he did with his own employees—especially if he'd already shared his concerns with them. Imagine what would happen if Bob came back to his own team after Max's meeting pretending to have "drunk the Kool-Aid" and changed his mind. His employees would either see him as spineless or suspect that he was lying, both of which create obvious problems.

Perhaps more importantly, disagreement is the first warning sign the organization has of trouble. The history of failed organizations is littered with situations in which people kept disagreements to themselves because, although they saw real problems, overwhelming social pressure required them to speak only the company line and never to say, "I don't think we should be doing this." The worries Bob has about Max's decision are probably based on real concerns, and those concerns need to be watched—not avoided, minimized, or turned into taboo topics.

So Bob is allowed, even encouraged, to say to his team, "Here's what we decided, although I personally disagree with this." Bob is allowed to continue to seek contrary evidence. Bob is even free to ask his employees to watch for contrary evidence. If new information arises, Bob is free to bring it back to Max's team in the form of another OSIR Report. The team is always Iterating, and no decision is "final." But every decision must proceed *without sabotage*.

The message from the boss—both from Max to Bob and from Bob to his employees—is clear and consistent: your first priority is full implementation of the decision. *Seeking contrary evidence is a distant second priority*. If you discover new information, we want to hear it. But if we find out you've done anything to subvert the decision, you will be held accountable. We do not sabotage each other in this organization. We win by working in coordination with each other, which means we all take turns doing things we personally disagree with—and this is a decision we have made together.

If you think all of this requires a certain level of maturity from the people involved, in a way you're right. But if you're worrying that it requires a greater level of maturity than most people have, you can put your mind at ease. There's no reason to believe that Iterative organizations are populated exclusively by very mature or otherwise magical people. Rather, they're populated by ordinary people doing what ordinary people do—behaving according to the norms they observe in the culture around them. That's why these behaviors are governed by an agreement, or "contract," between all the team members. The way to encourage this behavior—the way to encourage any behavior—is by making it part of common process and common practice.

For this decision—as with all the decisions before it, and all that will come after it—Alice, Bob, and Cal will do their best to implement the plan, as they discussed it and in full coordination with each other. They'll watch for problems, and they'll raise any they find, but in the meantime they *will* take the next step in their Iteration.

## ——————— ACTIVITY ———————

Reflect on the presence or absence of 100% Implementation in your organization.

1. Consider the management team you run. To what extent do you have a Disagree and Commit contract in place? To what extent do team members follow through on your decisions, even if they don't personally agree? How can you improve the Disagree and Commit agreement among your direct reports?

2. Consider any direct reports of yours who run their own management teams. How might you encourage them to create or improve upon a Disagree and Commit contract in those forums?

3. To what extent do you and your peers have a Disagree and Commit contract in place? Do you all follow through on group decisions as made by your manager?

4. What do you do when you personally disagree with a decision made by your manager? How do you implement it with your direct reports? Do you communicate it using "we" or "they" language? How do you encourage or discourage the seeking of contrary information?

## Disciplined Meeting Management

Group Decision-Making means decisions that affect a group are made in the group—*only* in the group. People don't take shortcuts around the group to deal with a group issue. If they try, whomever they approach refers them back to the group.

We've been talking about this practice in the context of the Work PreView Meetings between a manager and his or her direct staff. But that's only one case. Group Decision-Making also applies to other Work PreView Meetings, like standing cross-functional forums. It even applies to special one-time meetings. Really, any meeting with the task of making or recommending resource allocation changes will need to use Group Decision-Making; such decisions generally involve multiple parts of the organization, so they must be made in the presence of *all* of those parts, not in isolation from any of them.

Let's go back to Max's team to see why that's important. Alice brought her OSIR Report asking for Cal's budget to the appropriate group—in this case, Max's Work PreView Meeting. She needed a ruling from Max about resources from Cal. In an Iterative organization, that's how she gets it.

Consider the alternative: What if Alice went directly to Max? She could try to talk him into giving her some of Cal's budget one-on-one. If Cal heard about this, he would no doubt also approach Max one-on-one in an effort to protect his interests. The results would be predictable—posturing, politics, conflict, and a whole lot of time wasted by everyone as Max ends up in a sort of dysfunctional-parenting role, refereeing a turf war between his team members.

Max knows better. He does have one-on-one meetings with his team; they're necessary for personnel issues, compensation discussions, requests for his advice—all things related to manag*ing* them. But if Alice were to make her request for Cal's budget in a one-on-one meeting, Max would simply refer her back to the group. "Submit an OSIR Report," he would say, "and if it's high-enough priority, I'll put it on our next agenda." Resource manage-*ment* happens in the group. This keeps the whole team focused on the priorities that affect it, keeps everything transparent, and keeps Max and other managers out of the referee business.

It also means that a lot of information is processed, and a lot of decisions are made, in meetings. Max's meeting—and all the other meetings—need to operate as efficiently and effectively as possible. That's why the fourth Core

Component of Group Decision-Making is Disciplined Meeting Management. This is *how* an Iterative organization makes good decisions in groups and makes them fast enough to be useful.

Although a lot of us hate them, meetings are where management happens. They're where work gets organized, and they're where behavior and cultural norms are trained and reinforced. Meetings are unavoidable in any organization because they're the only way to coordinate resources for action. The only difference in an Iterative organization is that they're used that way *intentionally*.

Remember that all of the Key Practices are just that—*Key* Practices— minimum requirements that enable an organization to Iterate. In this case there are four minimum requirements for Disciplined Meeting Management: Agenda, Group Dynamics, Problem-Solving Process, and Group Memory. If you're going to run a productive, forward-looking, Iterative management meeting, think of these as the four items at the top of your to-do list. No matter how much you have to do or what other tasks come up as a result of running your meetings, once you've defined purpose and membership (see Purpose and Membership on page 76), you'd better take care of these four things.

## AGENDA

As mundane as it sounds, every meeting needs an agenda—one that's both complete and prepublished. "Complete" means that it defines who will do what for each portion of the meeting and that it lists an expected outcome for each agenda item, or what's supposed to happen as a result of it. "Prepublished" means that all participants in the meeting have the agenda in their hands beforehand—ideally twenty-four hours beforehand—so that they can be prepared. When Max decides to put Alice's OSIR Report on the agenda, she needs to know that he's expecting to hear from her; that's the agenda item. And the whole group needs to know that he's planning to make a decision about her request for Cal's budget; that's the expected outcome. Putting this in front of everyone in advance is the only way to make sure each team member comes prepared to have the conversation.

**Meeting Title:** Max's Weekly Work PreView
**Meeting Objective:** Adjust resource allocations as needed

Meeting Details:
*(Date, Time, Location, Connection Information, Required & Optional Attendees)*

| Time | Item/ What | Owner/ Who | Format | Expected Outcome |
|------|-----------|-----------|--------|-----------------|
| 9:00 – 9:06 | Passdowns – info from above | Max | Presentation | Group understands new developments and adjustments to Max's plan & graphs |
| 9:06 – 9:15 (3 min ea) | Pragmatic Dashboard Review | Alice, Bob, Cal | Dashboard Presentations | Quick overview of forward-looking status for each of us |
| 9:15 – 9:30 | Orange B Variance | Alice | OSIR Report & Group Decision | Decide if adjustments needed due to variance in Orange B |
| 9:30 – 9:40 | Black Task Force Report | Bob/Hal | Presentation & Group Decision | Recommendation by task force and decision whether to approve |
| 9:40 – 9:50 | Opens | All | Open Discussion | Resolve or charter small issues & questions |
| 9:50 | Adjourn | Everyone please plan to stay until 10:00 to allow for café style discussions. | | |

*Prepared and distributed no less than 24 hours prior to the meeting.*

Sample agenda: Work PreView Meeting.

## GROUP DYNAMICS

Good group dynamics means balanced participation from your team members: ideally, no one person will dominate the discussion, and no one will be completely disengaged. This is critical in management meetings; since each person represents one part of the organization and one part of the resources, the withdrawal or shutting out of one person equates to the removal of one whole section of the organization.

In reality, some people are more verbal than others, and levels of interaction vary. It's not uncommon for one person to do most of the talking while someone else seems completely distracted. Such situations can—and should—be addressed by someone playing a facilitative role in the meeting. The leader, or any member designated as the facilitator, can actively redirect conversation from those who are more verbal to those who are more withdrawn. But to put all the responsibility on one leader or facilitator is to absolve everyone else of his or her own responsibility. In reality, maintaining balanced participation is everyone's job.

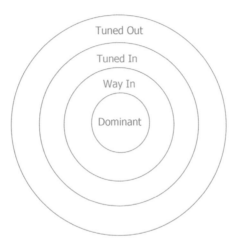

The Hill of Influence.

The Hill of Influence is a tool each person can use to notice his or her own level of participation in a meeting and a tool the leader or facilitator can use to reflect it back to the whole team. It's like a mirror for group dynamics that helps everyone notice what's really going on.

To create one, simply draw four concentric circles that represent a hill, as seen from the top in a topographical view. Any team member who's doing all the talking—*dominating* the discussion—would be noted as being at the top of the hill, in the center. Going down the hill are progressively lower levels of engagement: *tuned way in* means being engaged and actively conversing; *tuned in* means actively listening but making fewer comments; *tuned out* indicates a low level of engagement; and finally, at the bottom of the hill, *tuned way out* represents a state of complete distraction.

You can use the model to take your own notes about team members, like a snapshot of any given point in a meeting. But to put responsibility back in attendees' hands, use it as a meeting debriefing tool. Draw the circles on a flip chart or whiteboard, and give the team members sticky notes bearing names or initials. Ask team members to place their own names on the spot that corresponds to their overall level of participation throughout the meeting. Then ask them to check each other's placements. This will quickly engender a conversation, both about *actual* participation and about *perception* of engagement. You'll quickly bring out imbalances and open the door for constructive feedback among members. And if you repeat the exercise over several meetings, you'll find that it becomes more common for team members to self-correct in real time—quieting themselves so others can contribute, speaking up without invitation, or directly asking more reserved colleagues for their opinions.

The closer you can get your Group Decision-Making meeting to operating in an *equitable norm state*—meaning a state in which everyone is either "tuned in" (actively listening) or "tuned way in" (contributing appropriately)—the better. That way, the expertise and information you need are shared readily instead of being held hostage by accidental imbalances between levels of contribution.

## PROBLEM-SOLVING PROCESS

If group dynamics are about balancing levels of contribution, a problem-solving process is about ensuring that those well-balanced discussions reach a useful conclusion.

You can visualize any group's problem-solving process as a map with a sort of hourglass shape, made up of two distinct sections that the team moves through. Representing it this way helps remind us of two things—first, what needs to happen at each point in the process and, second, how much agreement or disagreement we can expect among group members as it does.

Notice that the entire upper portion of the model is concerned with the *facts*—the data and things people know to be true. At the start of the discussion—at the top—the lines on the left and right sides are close together, indicating agreement that there *is* a situation or condition needing improvement. Moving down the model from there, the lines separate. Invariably, as soon as the discussion starts, you realize people have different facts and different ideas about what the issue *really* is. That divergence is appropriate—the team needs to get all the facts on the table, and they won't agree much as they begin. Notice, though, how the outer lines converge again near the middle of the map. At that point, the team is coming together for the first time on a shared understanding: they have a real problem statement and a shared data set regarding what is true about it.

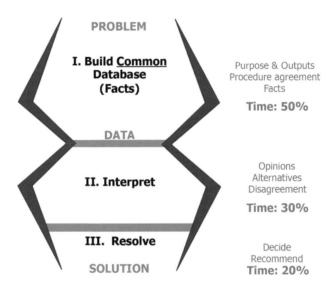

Group problem-solving process.

Now (and not sooner), the team is poised to enter the second phase of the conversation: *interpretation*. Again, the lines on both sides move farther apart; faced with the question of *what the data means*, everyone will start to disagree once again. This too is normal and to be expected—the team must work through this second round of disagreement. Once they have, when the hourglass narrows again at the bottom of the page, they will reach a conclusion about what should actually be done—the *solution*.

The fact that the model is drawn in equal halves is not accidental. Realistically, about 50% of the team's total time for the issue at hand should be spent in each half of the hourglass. That means half of the time is spent exclusively on facts—data and *what we know*—followed by the other half spent on *interpretation*. Within the interpretation section, the first 30% should be spent in disagreement over possible interpretations, with only the last 20% used for coming to agreement on a solution.

Imagine for a moment that Max has been tasked with investigating a downturn in company revenue. He gathers Alice, Bob, and Cal for a one-hour meeting, and he starts with a simple statement: "Revenues are lower than expected." For about thirty minutes the group concentrates on *information*—looking at revenue streams, trends over time, market data, and the like. This is necessary for the group to define a *real* problem statement—to go from "Revenues are lower than expected" to "We have enjoyed only 8% growth, relative to market averages of 12%, in three particular segments." Armed with such a specific problem statement, the group can then spend about eighteen minutes in discussion and disagreement over what the data *means*: What do the trends indicate? What are our strengths and weaknesses? What's likely to happen next? Only by the last twelve minutes or so of the meeting will the group be ready to narrow down and agree on recommended solutions.

Notice the implication here: if Max doesn't think twelve minutes will be enough for the group to come to agreement on specific recommendations, *he should schedule more time overall*. It's tempting to shortchange parts of this process—to save time by glossing over certain sections. But if the meeting doesn't give team members time to come to *two* agreements—first on the facts and then on the solution—it will devolve into a forum in which each member advocates for his or her opinion, with the leader refereeing the debate and picking the winner. But with each potential solution based only on the understanding of one team member, none of the options available in the debate will be as good as what the team could have come up with had the problem-solving process been followed.

## GROUP MEMORY

The last item on your list of must-haves for Disciplined Meeting Management is group memory. As the group works together, they need a shared visual reference for their work. After the meeting, that same visual reference should be made available as a record.

There are lots of ways to accomplish this. In a live, in-person meeting, the easiest is probably some combination of flip charts and a projection system showing notes being typed up. In a virtual meeting, flip charts aren't an option, but plenty of online collaboration tools allow for screen sharing and shared markup. In reality, it doesn't matter whether it's a PowerPoint slide annotated by the group working online (as in the figure on page 84), an old-fashioned flip chart made in a conference room (as in the figure below), an Excel spreadsheet typed up by one person while everyone watches and suggests changes (as in the figure on page 100), or something else altogether. All that matters is that the group be allowed to create it and see it *together*.

Once it's created, it should be made available to meeting participants afterward *in the same format*. This is good news for anyone who thinks part of his or her job is to type up flip charts or edit and reformat notes taken on the fly: don't do it. Simply take a picture or screenshot and send it to everyone. Though it may seem a bit less elegant, by presenting the same notes in the same visual layout, you'll help team members recall *exactly* what was discussed and decided and spare them the cognitive load of having to interpret typed-up notes they've never seen before. You'll also spare someone the editorial task of creating the notes nobody needs.

### ALICE'S OSIR
**Decisions:**
1. Alice gets $X (¼ of request) from Cal
2. Bob lends 2 heads to Alice from workweek 23-39
3. Bob reschedules Project X with Customer M
4. Message to Customer M is...

Outcome of group decision regarding Alice's OSIR Report: flip chart.

| | DECISION LOG | |
|---|---|---|
| WHO | WHAT | WHEN |
| Cal | Transfer $X to Alice from standard budget code XY-103 | WW22 |
| Bob | 2 heads (TBD) temp assign to Alice | WW23-39 |
| Bob | Reschedule Project X to 8 week delay | WW22 ASAP |
| Max | Customer M messaging RE: Project X slip | WW22 |

Outcome of group decision regarding Alice's OSIR Report: decision log spreadsheet.

Group memory may seem like a small detail, at least compared with publishing an agenda, managing group dynamics, and using a good problem-solving process. And there's a reason it's fourth on the list: if you run a meeting with multiple areas for improvement, work on the others first, in the order presented, starting with the agenda. But once you've got those where they need to be, you'll find there's no substitute for a good group memory system—both for helping the process move along when you're together and for making sure your agreements stick afterward.

▶ WATCH THE VIDEOS!

If you want to refresh your memory on the four components of Disciplined Meeting Management or share the concepts with others, visit **IterateNow.com** and use your free account to watch the videos on each: *Agendas Turbo-Charge Meetings; Group Dynamics and the Hill of Influence; Problem-Solving Process: Solve It Once!;* and *Use Group Memory to Make Your Decisions Stick.*

For any management meeting you run—or any that you're a part of—Disciplined Meeting Management maximizes your chances of getting to useful output, time and again. Given a clearly defined purpose and the right set of attendees (see the sidebar on page 76), detailed agendas let everyone come prepared, group dynamics ensure interactions are balanced, a clear problem-solving process leads those interactions to useful conclusions, and group memory supports implementation of what's been decided. Taken together, the four elements of Disciplined Meeting Management make your meetings as painless and efficient as possible.

That's important, because much of the work of Iteration happens in problem-solving and Work PreView Meetings of all kinds—like the one in which Alice presented her OSIR Report. Maintaining good discipline around how they're run isn't terribly difficult, but it is critical in enabling the organization to Iterate.

## HOW TO FIX A BAD MEETING

Agendas and group memory are easy to spot when missing and easy to implement. If they're in place but a meeting still feels redundant, tense, or just plain bad, there's probably a problem with either group dynamics or the group's problem-solving process. To diagnose the problem, ask yourself two simple questions.

First, "Is my meeting functional or dysfunctional?" In a functional meeting, there's a sense of balance in the interactions and engagement and a feeling of mutual respect. Everyone interacts with whomever he or she needs to as the meeting goes along. In a dysfunctional meeting, there's more domination and disengagement. People take over or cliques form, and others don't care. There's often a feeling of disrespect, a sense of not valuing or even listening to each other's contributions.

Second, ask, "Is my meeting Iterative or repetitive?" In an Iterative meeting, it feels as if the group is usually taking some next step. There's a sense of progress, even though the work may be difficult. In a repetitive meeting, it feels as if the group is solving the same problem again and again. There's a frustrating sense of redundancy and ineffectiveness, like constantly falling back to the start or being caught in a loop going nowhere.

Ask the first question first because if your meeting is dysfunctional, it can't possibly be Iterative. To move from dysfunctional to functional, work on group dynamics—on having the right people at the table, on having good participation ground rules, and on having internal or external facilitation to help people stay engaged.

How? Ask: "Do we have the right people at this meeting to get the work done? Do we have some ground rules on participation?" (Here's one possibility: when one person shares some information, somebody else has to restate it in different words so it's clear that the whole group understood what the first person said.) It may be that the group needs facilitation—possibly even from an external source, if things are bad.

Once that's solved, move on to the second question. If your group feels repetitive instead of Iterative, get to work on your group's problem-solving process. Make sure the team is fully defining the problem before setting to work on solutions. Ensure that they're looking at multiple possible options, and ensure that they're considering the broader context of implementation *before* making any final decisions.

How? Ask: "What is our clear definition of the problem?" Make sure everyone agrees on that definition before the conversation turns to possible solutions. Then, when it is time to enter the solution space, ask: "Are we looking at *all* options? What else is possible?" Once a small number of options are under serious consideration, invite the group to broaden the context. Ask: "How would doing each of these affect the others involved who aren't in this room? Do we need to consult with any of them?"

Group dynamics and a problem-solving process don't solve every group problem, but they do help with a lot of them. Get them right, and you'll have a good chance of turning your bad meeting into a better one.

## ▶ WATCH THE VIDEO!

Your copy of this book includes prepaid access to a library of videos, including *How to Fix a Bad Meeting*. You can watch the video now, then return to it later to refresh your memory or share concepts with others. Create your free account and watch any video, anytime, at **IterateNow.com**.

## ACTIVITY

Consider the meetings you attend as a manager.

1. Which have a clear purpose and the right membership? Which do not?

2. How strong is your practice of Disciplined Meeting Management in the meetings you run with your direct reports? With others? Consider each individually:

   - Agenda
   - Group dynamics
   - Problem-solving process
   - Group memory

3. Choose one area of the four that would be most helpful to your regular meetings with your direct reports. Review the pertinent content in the chapter, and watch the related video. Then, make an action plan to improve your next meeting. Be specific about what you will do and when—then notice the result.

4. For anyone you manage who manages *other managers,* what insight do you have into the extent to which they run their own staff meetings using Disciplined Meeting Management? Which of the four areas do you think might be most beneficial to each of them? Consider each individually:

   - Agenda
   - Group dynamics
   - Problem-solving process
   - Group memory

5. How strong do you think your manager is in running his or her meeting with you and your peers? Are there any improvements you could assist with or recommend in any of the four areas? Consider each individually:

   - Agenda
   - Group dynamics
   - Problem-solving process
   - Group memory

## SUMMARY: GROUP DECISION-MAKING

The Iterative organization can only make the best decision possible every step of the way by benefiting from group intelligence; Group Decision-Making helps the management team do just that. The Group Consultative Process produces the best decisions possible. Fully Commissioned Decisions and 100% Implementation ensure that those decisions are turned into action. And Disciplined Meeting Management supports both decisions and implementation by making sure the meetings run well and the decisions are clearly documented.

---

### ▶ WATCH THE VIDEO!

Your copy of this book includes prepaid access to a library of videos, including *How to Optimize Group Decision-Making*. You can watch the video now, then return to it later to refresh your memory or share concepts with others. Create your free account and watch any video, anytime, at **IterateNow.com**.

---

### ──── ACTIVITY ────

It's time to bring the concept of Group Decision-Making to your organization. As always, remember to separate in your own mind the question of how to practice the behaviors from the question of whether or not to teach others about the labels.

1. Plan a group decision for your team of direct reports, in which you'll be the decider.

   - Who on your team will present the request for a decision?

   - Will you need to coach him or her to make an OSIR Report that includes a recommendation? Do so beforehand.

   - How much time will you need for the discussion of facts? For the discussion of solutions? How will you keep the discussion from devolving into politics and advocacy?

- How will you know when it's time to stop listening and make a decision?
- How will you remember to commission your decision with the team?
- How will you set up the team for 100% Implementation— to have a Disagree and Commit agreement—before the presentation?
- What other elements of Disciplined Meeting Management may become important? Consider agenda, group dynamics, problem-solving process, and group memory. Do you need a plan for one or more of these areas?

2. Hold your meeting and note the results. If possible, debrief with your team to get their impressions, too.

3. If you manage people who manage *other managers*, begin discussing Group Decision-Making with them. Explore the ways in which they make decisions on their own teams. Try to determine whether they're taking maximum advantage of the intelligence of those teams or if they're using a decision-making methodology that is less effective. Encourage them to be intentional about how they make group decisions.

CHAPTER 6

# LINKED TEAMS

You can't bake a pie one slice at a time.
–WILLIAM R. DANIELS

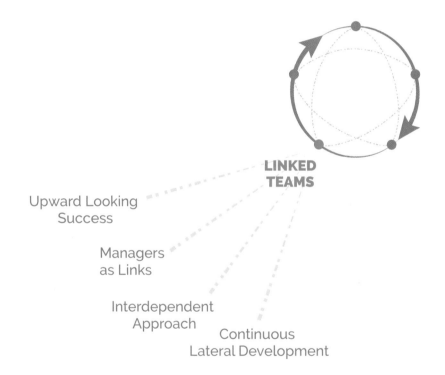

LINKED
TEAMS

Upward Looking
Success

Managers
as Links

Interdependent
Approach

Continuous
Lateral Development

We need to talk about Cal.

Cal is human, and humans can be protective and defensive. And Alice just gave an OSIR Report asking Max to take away money from Cal and give it to her.

Of course, this isn't actually Cal's money. It's a *resource*—a resource the organization assigned to Cal's output because that seemed like the optimal use of it. As outside observers, it's easy for us to say, "Look, if it's better for the organization to move the money from Cal to Alice, then that's what the organization should do."

We're right about that. And yet . . . If you've seen humans become protective and defensive, and if you were paying close attention to the section about Disciplined Meeting Management, you should be worried. Max publishes the agenda for his meeting twenty-four hours in advance, which means Cal gets a full day of advance notice about Alice making overtures for his funds. That's a full day to call together his team, circle the wagons, call in all the favors he can, and put together his best defense.

Never mind the amount of time that will burn for Cal, his team, and their teams. And never mind the fact that Max is diligent in refusing to have the conversation with Cal one-on-one before the meeting. Nothing prevents Cal from coming into Max's Work PreView Meeting, guns blazing, ready to make a preemptive strike as soon as the last word of Alice's OSIR Report is out of her mouth.

And why shouldn't he? "Alice," he might say politely, "I like you and all . . . but you're not going to take *my* money." In some organizations, this might even be labeled as a *desirable* management behavior—watching out for one's team, protecting one's interests.

The thing is, there's no way to produce Iteration if, once resources are assigned, they can never be moved.

To solve this problem, we need to move on from Group Decision-Making to the next of our Key Management Practices: **Linked Teams**. This consists of four Core Components which together define how each manager links his or her part of the organization to the rest: **Upward Looking Success** explains how success is defined, **Managers as Links** defines the role of each manager in achieving it, **Interdependent Approach** explains how managers work together to achieve it, and **Continuous Lateral Development** ensures that the management team is always developing to stay ready for the *next* challenge.

# Upward Looking Success

We start with Upward Looking Success, which is, in some sense, little more than a psychological trick.

Most managers conceptualize their job using a standard organization chart. You can't blame them; it's the picture they're shown, over and over, of how everything fits together. Here's what that would look like for Alice. She works for Max trying to produce the Orange result, which consists of Orange A, B, and C. So she assigns A to Dan, B to Ed, and C to Fay.

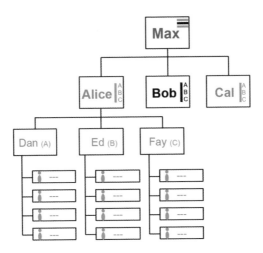

Organization chart representation of Alice's organization and relationship to Max.

According to the North American Management Model, if Alice manages her group well, she works one-on-one with each of its members on a clear definition of success. She lets them know what they should do, how they'll be measured, and how they can predict whether they'll be successful or not. She's specific with Dan about the criteria for A, with Ed about the criteria for B, and with Fay about the criteria for C. In this approach, each team member knows exactly what to bring back to Alice to be successful, and it's Alice's job to knit those results together so that she can bring Orange ABC to Max.

That sounds good, right? Nobody would argue against clear goals and success criteria. But what happens when Alice tells the managers who work for her, "Each of you focus on your part of the work, and I'll focus on putting the pieces together"?

One thing that happens is, before long, Dan, Ed, and Fay start approaching Alice with conversations that sound like this: "Boss, *here's what I need.* I need more money to hit my targets. I need more staff. I need help from someone else in the organization who won't give it to me without your say-so. Please help me by getting me what I need."

Of course, at the same time, Max is asking Alice, "*How are things going?*" (Bosses do that.) "Is everything progressing? Will you hit your targets? Is everything on schedule?"

To get an answer, Alice asks Dan, Ed, and Fay, "*How are things going?*" (Bosses do that, mostly because *their* bosses are doing it.) "Is everything progressing? Will you hit your targets? Is everything on schedule?"

The result is an ongoing series of one-on-one conversations between Alice and each of her group members, in which "*Here's what I need*" meets "*How are things going?*"

Alice asks Dan or Ed or Fay, "So, how's it going?" and they all reply the same way: "I'll tell you how things are going. If you can't get me what I need, I'm not going to be able to deliver what you're asking for."

This puts Alice on the receiving end of a large number of requests, all framed as mission critical—and she has to figure out, alone, how to respond. Should she escalate the need to Max? Should she push the issue back on her employee to resolve? Should she ask her peers for help? Should she simply not worry about this particular issue? And what about cases where she needs to instruct one of her employees to support a peer—and then her employee comes back demanding that the peer be the one to give support? With every problem framed as critical and every employee arguing the priority of his or her own work over the rest of what Alice cares about, it's a stressful and inefficient life for Alice—one in which she's mostly worrying about what's *not* getting done and refereeing resource and turf wars between group members.

The solution—the psychological trick—is for Alice to *change the way she and her reports conceptualize their relationship,* for all of them to think of themselves not as a group but *as a team.* The difference is small but hugely important: each team has a single charter. From the first day they work together, Alice tells Dan, Ed, and Fay: "You each have your own goals and your own area of responsibility, but fundamentally we work *together* to achieve *my* output plan, Orange ABC. *We are the Orange ABC Team.*"

The leader's VSO is the team's VSO. Everyone has his or her own goals, but in the end everyone succeeds or fails based on whether or not *the whole team* succeeds or fails. That's Upward Looking Success. It can't be captured by organization charts because those only show relationships between *individuals*. The Iterative organization is defined by relationships between *teams*. Individual work is important, but individuals work in teams on the output their leader owes to the next level above them—the output defined by the leader's plan. Alice runs the Orange ABC team, which delivers its output to Max's Orange/Black/Green team.

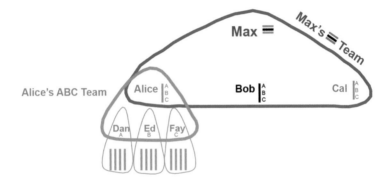

Linked Teams representation of Alice's organization and relationship to Max.

---

### ▶ WATCH THE VIDEO!

Your copy of this book includes prepaid access to a library of videos, including *Linked Teams: How and Why to Make Your Group into a Team*. You can watch the video now, then return to it later to refresh your memory or share concepts with others. Create your free account and watch any video, anytime, at **IterateNow.com**.

---

This same principle, at the next level up, solves our potential problem with Cal. Max runs his team with Upward Looking Success too. Alice is responsible for Orange A, B, and C—that's her VSO and the basis for her Pragmatic Dashboards. Bob has a VSO and dashboards too. He's responsible for Black A, B, and C. And Cal is responsible for Green A, B, and C. This all rolls up to Max's VSO—Orange, Black, and Green, which is properly abstracted at Max's level.

Those are their *individual* responsibilities, but Max gives them all the same message over and over again: "We are the Orange/Black/Green *Team*. We exist to achieve *my* VSO—Orange, Black, and Green. You're each responsible for doing your part—Cal, you have Green, but you all succeed together when we achieve *my* higher-level goals. If we don't achieve the whole plan, you've all failed. Please try not to fail."

"*We succeed or fail together.*" That's Max's message, and the implications are enormous: if Alice hits all of her Orange targets but Cal doesn't hit his Green ones, both Alice and Cal have failed—and so has Bob. And if Cal succeeds at accomplishing Green but Alice doesn't complete Orange, Cal has failed as badly as if he hadn't completed his own work on Green—and so has Bob. That's the message of Upward Looking Success.

Although it's a little scary for all involved—or maybe *because* it is—Upward Looking Success is tremendously powerful in encouraging proactive resource sharing and tearing down silos. Once team members see their success as *combined* instead of *isolated*, they start looking for ways to share with each other instead of finding excuses not to. It's not uncommon in Iterative organizations to see a manager asking, encouraging, or even *pushing* a peer to take some help. Nobody wants to fail.

Because of this, Alice, Bob, and Cal are in the habit of sharing resources. Any request for help from one of them—whether it's for money, funds, or equipment—is met with openness and support from the others. It has been this way for as long as Cal has been a member of Max's team. That's why there's nothing particularly new or uniquely offensive about Alice making an OSIR Report in which she asks for some of Cal's budget: the idea of "supporting his peers" isn't just a feel-good concept for Cal that's at odds with the way he's managed. It's *fundamental* to the way he's managed, to how Max operates—and Cal knows it.

Does this mean Cal happily complies when Alice asks for his funds? He might, if he has a surplus of funds and agrees that Alice's work is the best use of it. But it's more likely that he won't be happy about Alice's request at all.

Remember, Cal is best positioned to understand the *real* impact of taking funds away from Green. He's probably going to argue against it. At the very least, it's his responsibility to explain clearly to the team what the real impact to Green will be if they decide to follow Alice's recommendation. Max encourages and requires this; he needs that information to make an intelligent trade-off decision.

Upward Looking Success doesn't change the fact that Cal is largely responsible for Green—and that Alice is largely responsible for Orange. But it does change their *orientation* toward each other. For both Alice *and* Cal, it's not about Orange versus Green, it's about the best way to achieve Max's plan of Orange, Black, *and* Green.

Their focus is *upward*, not sideways. Alice asks for Cal's money in her OSIR Report because she believes it's better for the broader success of the group. If Cal objects, it'll be because he has a different idea of how to best achieve that shared success. Any debate between them is a debate over what's best for Max's plan—Orange, Black, *and* Green.

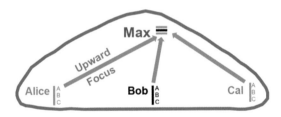

Alice, Bob, and Cal focus on Max's output plan.

Remember, people in Iterative organizations are neither extra mature nor otherwise magical. They still have that reptile part of the brain—that part that wants to protect itself from harm and failure. It's just that, thanks to the signals around them—mostly common process and common practice— the line between success and failure is drawn a little differently. The failure they're avoiding is *the failure of the team*, because the failure of the team is the failure of the individual.

There's also no requirement that all managers have a sunny disposition. If Cal is a person who's inclined to complain, he'll still complain. But his complaint will be different in an Iterative organization. Instead of "I can't believe Alice wants me to sacrifice *my* Green output because of *her* poor planning on

Orange," it'll sound like "Oh, great, now *our* Orange/Black/Green output is at risk, and I'm the only one who can help."

Iteration involves constant evaluation and constant adjustment. It really is true: the budget assigned to Cal is nothing more than a resource that the organization should optimize. Wherever that resource was originally assigned, as new information arises, intelligent corrections will need to be made. And if there is a trade-off to be made between Orange and Green, there is no better person in the organization to decide than Max, there are no better people for Max to consult than Alice and Cal, and there is no better way for Max to decide than by consulting with them on what would serve the higher-level goal.

That way, instead of competing, Alice and Cal are optimizing. Instead of refereeing, Max is learning and deciding. And instead of blindly following a plan that no longer matches reality, the organization is Iterating.

## ───── ACTIVITY ─────

Reflect on the Upward Looking Success that exists in your organization.

1. Consider your direct reports. To what extent do you practice Upward Looking Success, encouraging and requiring your direct reports to work together on your output commitment? To what extent do you encourage them to work in silos on their own separate output?

2. What could you do to drive a greater degree of Upward Looking Success into the management team you run?

3. If you manage people who manage *other managers*, to what extent do those people practice Upward Looking Success with their teams? How might you encourage them to improve the practice?

4. To what extent does your manager practice Upward Looking Success, encouraging and requiring you and your peers to work together on his or her output commitment? To what extent does he or she encourage you to work in silos on your separate output?

## Managers as Links

It's a strangely two-sided thing, this idea of Upward Looking Success. In one view, it's obvious, intuitive, and logical: *of course* we want the organization optimizing its output toward higher-level goals rather than having different departments in silos, wasting time and effort competing with each other. And Max certainly doesn't lose any quality of life by *not* refereeing turf wars between his direct reports. At first glance, managing the Orange/Black/Green team *as a team* with a single charter, rather than a collection of individual direct reports, is all upside for Max.

That goes for Alice, too. She runs her team as the Orange ABC team on the same principle. Dan, Ed, and Fay all succeed to the extent to which Alice's VSO, Orange, is accomplished. There's no such thing as doing Orange A at the expense of Orange B. Dan can't succeed at Ed's or Fay's expense—they can only succeed together. Again, this looks pretty good for Alice.

Upward Looking Success is great when you're looking *down* the organizational hierarchy. The notion of getting your direct reports to cooperate to produce your plan sounds perfect. That's what they should do because you're their boss and that's what you want them to do!

But what about when you look up or sideways? What do you see when you look at your boss or your peers?

As Shakespeare said, there's the rub. In that direction, Upward Looking Success seems a whole lot less attractive. The notion of your boss forcing you to coordinate your work with your peers instead of turning you loose to succeed or fail on your own—well, that's not so great. Surely, you would much rather be turned loose with a goal and a bunch of resources to manage however you see fit. You don't want your success coupled to the success of your peers; for all you know, they're not as smart as you are. You deserve autonomy!

This sounds a little funny, but it's also extremely serious. Many of the North American Management Model's largest misconceptions rear their ugly heads when confronted with Upward Looking Success: for example, the idea that your job as a manager is to advocate for and protect your people *against* the organization at large—and that your manager should be protecting you; the idea that the way you manage your people is your business and not anyone else's; and the idea that the more people, money, and resources you can secure under your control, the more successful you are. If you take any one of these philosophical concepts and look at it in the light of day, it flies in the face of common sense—at least if the organization's goal is to coordinate people working on complex outputs. And yet, as practices, these behaviors and others like them don't die easily.

For an organization to Iterate, managers at all levels need to be clear on what it really means to be a manager. The second Core Component of Linked Teams, Managers as Links, defines that job.

Managers as Links is a three-word definition of the *real* role of the manager: to *link* his or her part of the organization to the whole. It's this description of management that managers bear in mind, constantly, as they evaluate their own actions. And it's this description of management that their supervisors use to evaluate them. When Max sits down to consider how Alice is performing, he doesn't ask himself whether or not she is convincing in arguing for her function at the expense of the others, whether she smoothly influences people to come around to her way of thinking, or whether she buckles down and finishes Orange in isolation from the rest of the group. He asks himself whether Alice does a good job *coordinating* her Orange ABC team's output with the rest of his team.

Alice's Orange ABC team and Max's Orange/Black/Green team are Linked Teams—and Alice is the link. That's how Max evaluates her, and she knows that's how he evaluates her.

One of the reasons this can be a difficult pill to swallow is that it takes away some of the Old West, "guy on a horse riding off into the sunset," "give me what I need and I'll get it done," made-for-TV notion of management. There are no lone heroes managing complex, coordinated work. Managers as Links means making it clear to the managers who work for you that, whoever they are, at whatever level of management, they're part of an interconnected larger system, and *they have to act like it*. Because if they don't, they literally sever the connection between their part of the organization and the rest.

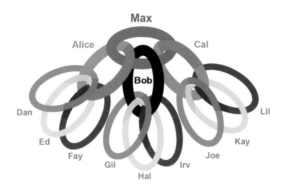

Each manager links his or her part of the organization to the whole.

No doubt, getting yourself and the managers working for you used to this idea can be the hard part. The good news is that once everyone comes to grips with this, it can actually be a *more* engaging description of the management role. Helping a team to succeed *along with* everyone else—instead of *despite* everyone else—can be both more challenging and more fulfilling.

One might also suggest that how any individual manager *feels* about his or her role as defined by Managers as Links is, frankly, beside the point. The fact is, it's true whether we like it or not. Anyone who manages part of an organization *does* link that part to the whole, and it *is* better for everyone if the link is strong. The old cliché is true: the whole chain is only as strong as its weakest link. Being interconnected *is* the job. The only question is, how good is each manager at doing it?

## LINKED TEAMS AND COMPENSATION

One frequent objection to Upward Looking Success and Managers as Links is that salary and bonus structures don't support them. "We can talk about teamwork all we want," the argument goes, "but people do what they're paid for, and here we're paid for individual work instead of team-work." In some companies, you can also add, "and our bonuses are based on higher-level results over which we have no control."

Does the pay and bonus structure have to be defined a certain way for an organization to Iterate?

Ideally, there would be some alignment. And if you have any say in how your company gives performance incentives and output-based bonuses, you'd be well advised to study the concept of Linked Teams carefully. Managers as Links can be written into the standard performance expectations of all managers: if Bob chooses to decouple Gil, Hal, Irv, and their teams from the organization—if he breaks his link by refusing to collaborate or share resources with Alice and Cal (see the figure on page 117)—that choice certainly shouldn't be rewarded. Similarly, Upward Looking Success can be incorporated into a bonus structure: to the extent that it's possible to give bonuses to Alice, Bob, and Cal based on *Max's* results, that's the best approach, at least at senior levels.

Real life, however, is seldom ideal. Most managers live inside a pre-defined compensation system over which they have little design influence. Does that mean Iterative Management is impossible?

Fortunately, it doesn't. As *users* of the compensation system, managers almost always have latitude in how they evaluate their direct reports. And even outside of that, managers exert tremendous influence on reports simply through the requests they make and feedback they give, day in and day out, year in and year out.

If you're a manager who can't redesign your compensation system, you can still set expectations—and request and require behaviors—consistent with Upward Looking Success and Managers as Links. You can tell your team, "We succeed or fail together." You can tell them their job is to *collaborate* to achieve *your* output plan and that you'll personally view *all of them* as successful, or not, based on those *shared* results. And you can tell them their role is to be a *link* and that your assessment of their performance is strongly influenced by the extent to which they *connect and coordinate*, rather than isolate and protect, their part of the organization and the work it does.

The truth is, no matter how they're designed, compensation systems are always tremendously challenging. Do what you can with yours, but don't be fooled: there are other, equally important ways to encourage your part of the organization to Iterate.

---------- ACTIVITY ----------

Consider the extent to which the managers in your organization play their role as defined by Managers as Links.

1. Reflect on the managers who work for you. To what extent do you require them to link their part of the organization to your broader whole? How do you help or encourage them to play that role? What do you do that makes it more difficult for them to play that role?

2. To what extent do you, as a manager, link your part of the organization to the broader system of your manager's area of responsibility? What makes you better at serving as that link? What makes you worse at it?

3. To what extent does your manager serve as the link between his or her part of the organization and the rest of it? To what extent does he or she set that expectation for you? Are other, contradictory expectations placed on you? Do those find their way to your direct reports?

# Interdependent Approach

As you read about a manager's work being interconnected with the work of his or her peers, you may feel a little uncomfortable: after all, I'm basically saying every manager is both (a) individually accountable for the execution of his or her own output commitment and (b) jointly accountable with peers to the manager's higher-level output commitment—even when (b) conflicts with (a). Is this another psychological trick? Is it a fundamental conflict that can't be resolved?

As it turns out, it's neither. It's simply the third Core Component of Linked Teams: Interdependent Approach.

*Interdependence* is the third of three progressive levels in a simple model of human maturity. To understand what it means, it's useful to look at the previous levels, even to think of them as tangible *steps*—three rungs on a ladder that leads to maturity.

The first rung is *dependence*. In human development, this corresponds to an infant or toddler—one who depends on an external source for survival. In the workplace, on an individual level, this might be an employee who is totally reliant on his or her manager for everything: salary, career, direction, happiness, and the like. On a group level, it might look like a group or department that's totally dependent on one customer: getting all of their feedback from them, allowing them to direct activity and strongly influence prices, always prioritizing their requests, and so on.

Dependence isn't ideal, for obvious reasons. So personally and professionally, the goal is to step up from dependence to *independence*. As the name suggests, the second rung is in many ways the opposite of the first. In human development, this corresponds to a teenager rebelling against his or her parents and claiming sovereignty (and then driving off in the family car). In the workplace, on an individual level, this might be an employee who says, "I don't care about my boss or my peers. I'm not going to do what they want; I can always find another job." On a group level, it might be a group or department that rejects customer feedback unilaterally: "We know what we're doing, and we don't want to be distracted from our expertise. It doesn't matter what you want."

While it's better in many ways than dependence—and significantly more pervasive as a general philosophy in Western society and in the North American Management Model—independence has some serious drawbacks. Most importantly, it's not particularly realistic. The teenager's life is funded by the parents; the employee only has so many job prospects; the company may not truly understand its market. Asserting independence to the detriment of collaborative relationships is problematic, especially in Iterative organizations trying to accomplish dynamic, highly complex work.

*Interdependence* is the top rung of the maturity ladder—it's a more complex view of the world. In human development, interdependence corresponds to an adult who is able to effectively navigate personal and professional relationships, recognizing when to assert his or her autonomy and when not to. In the workplace, on an individual level, it's the employee who makes a strong effort to meet the manager's needs without checking his or her brain at the door or becoming a sycophantic yes-man. On a group level, it's an organization that recognizes the complexity of its own relationship with multiple customers and competitors and attempts to learn as much as possible about those parties' relationships with each other.

Interdependent individuals and groups understand that they're part of a complex network in which their actions and the actions of others interrelate. They appreciate that most disagreements in that context require mutually beneficial resolutions that are more sophisticated than simply picking a winner and a loser. And they find that the word "or" is often replaced with the word "and" in both the definition of those issues and in their solutions.

An interdependent adult behaves autonomously *and* pays attention to guidelines imposed by family, employer, society, and culture.

An interdependent professional takes initiative in selecting employment and accepting work *and* is mindful of constraints—even conflicting ones—from supervisor, customer, employees, and the like.

An interdependent organization is able to represent itself fairly in a price negotiation with a customer *and* recognize that there's a broader relationship between the two entities that will be impacted by the result.

---

## FROM DEPENDENCE TO INTERDEPENDENCE

Managers often complain that their job is too much like babysitting and that their employees aren't mature enough. You can help your team, or its members, to become more mature by helping it move up the three rungs of maturity.

Start by recognizing where you are.

At *dependence*, you may notice a victim mentality. You'll hear comments like "So-and-so told me to do it, so I have no choice." Or you may detect a sense of sacrifice: "Our customer is forcing us to lower the price to save the business." Dependence typically comes with a sense of hopelessness, a feeling of being subject to forces beyond one's control.

At *independence*, you'll notice less victim mentality and more persecutor or rescuer. You might hear, "I'm not going to do what you want, and there's nothing you can do about it." Or "Everybody else is kind of thin-skinned, but *I'm* here to tell you how it's *really* going to be." You also may detect detachment or overconfidence, as in "I don't really care what my customer wants" or "I can always get a new job."

Once you know where you are, you can plan your next step upward.

To move from dependence to *independence*, focus on the value the individual or team has to offer. What strength, asset, or unique ability does the person or team bring to the table? To get away from victimhood, you'll need to move toward independence.

Just don't stop when you get there! To move from independence to *interdependence*, preserve the focus on the value that "I" or "we" offer, but balance it with a recognition of what the other groups or parties bring in return. Here's where you'll hopefully start to see what's called "non-dualistic thinking"—solutions that contain more "and" than "or."

Maybe it's no longer about making a decision between conflict resolution *or* asserting our needs, because the group finds a way to do both. Or maybe it's not a conflict between collaboration *or* negotiation, because the individual becomes comfortable doing both at once. Connecting seemingly contradictory activities is an indication of more mature, more complex thinking.

As you encourage your team up the ladder, remember: they will have a hard time getting ahead of you. If *you're* stuck at dependence, they'll be stuck there with you. And if you're stuck at independence, they'll be stuck there too. Be sure to move yourself up first, and then bring your employees and team with you.

## ▶ WATCH THE VIDEO!

Your copy of this book includes prepaid access to a library of videos, including *From Dependence to Interdependence: Make Your Team and Yourself More Mature*. You can watch the video now, then return to it later to refresh your memory or share concepts with others. Create your free account and watch any video, anytime, at **IterateNow.com**.

In short, to be interdependent is to say "and" when you're tempted to say "or." But what does it mean for an Iterative organization to take an Interdependent *Approach*?

Since Iterative organizations aren't populated with people who are significantly more mature than everyone else (or with magical people)—and since we need managers in those organizations to behave at the top rung of the maturity ladder—the environment must *encourage* highly mature behavior. The common processes and common practices used day in and day out in management have to encourage everyone, all the time, to behave as maturely as possible. That's what's meant by Interdependent *Approach.*

Look how Max handles this with Alice, Bob, and Cal. Alice is accountable to accomplish all of Orange *and* to coordinate it with the rest of Max's team. Bob has to ensure all the Black work gets done *and* delay his work by offering resources to his peers if it makes sense to do so. Cal has to explain the impact of a budget transfer away from Green *and* advocate for Max's higher-level priorities. These three individuals are interdependent—they have to work both independently of each other *and* in coordination. And they know it because Max reminds them—by saying so directly and by how he runs his team.

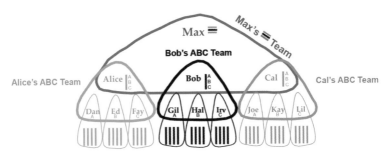

Max's entire organization, represented as Linked Teams.

Realistically, this is another one of those things that, though the individuals involved may not like it, is true anyway. Imagine that Max is the CEO of a company that makes products. Alice owns sales and marketing, Bob owns development, and Cal owns production. Ask yourself: Has Max succeeded if the company gets sales contracts for products and develops them but fails to produce them? If production is behind, and sales and marketing are ahead, and Max *doesn't* redirect resources to compensate, wouldn't we call him incompetent? And if the organization fails in that manner—if it goes out of business with Alice and Bob ahead and Cal behind—does Alice end up any less unemployed than Cal?

Alice, Bob, and Cal are interdependent, whether they like it or not. And they are interdependent, whether Max is CEO of the whole company, president of a huge division, or the manager of one tiny group. The concept of the Interdependent Approach simply means that they all know it, and they all act like it.

Let's be honest, though. This does add a level of complexity to resource allocation decisions. Remember the resolution of Alice's OSIR Report? Think about how many parts it has—Cal's budget, Bob's headcount, Bob's Project X, customer messaging. And that's only the *outcome* of the discussion. Imagine what else came into play while they were talking through their options: How much budget can Cal really afford to transfer? Should Bob take resources off Project X or Project Y? Is there a different piece of work Alice or Cal could delay? What are the trade-offs? What are the relative values? How can they still get *everything* done?

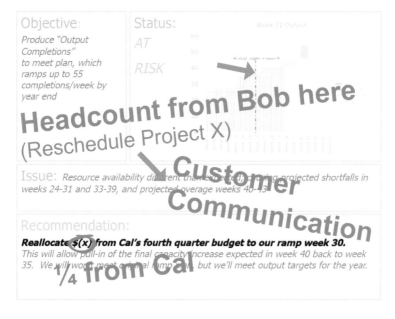

Outcome of group decision regarding Alice's OSIR Report: annotated slide.

An Interdependent Approach requires a degree of tolerance for this sort of complicated problem-solving. One of the best pieces of advice for managers wondering how best to succeed in Iterative organizations is to *embrace complexity*. That's what Alice, Bob, Cal, and Max do; they don't get scared off by multifaceted solutions. While their peers in non-Iterative organizations say, "One thing at a time," Iterative managers dive into the complexity head-on.

Please understand, this doesn't prevent them from seeking the simplest solution possible. Simplest is usually best, and they know it. Managers like Alice, Bob, Cal, and Max never create change or complexity for its own sake. They're fully cognizant of the impact to their teams of their decisions, and they don't make them lightly. But at the same time, they don't force simplicity when complexity produces a better result, and they don't hesitate to change course, in small ways and big ways, when the facts suggest they should. Because if you can't slow down, speed up, or change direction, you're not Iterating. And that's as true for your organization as it moves toward its goals as it is for you as you walk to your car.

## ACTIVITY

Reflect on the extent to which managers in your organization take an Interdependent Approach.

1. In what ways are your direct reports *interdependent* in collaborating to create the output that *you* owe to the organization? In what ways do they recognize and act on that interdependence? In what ways do you, as their supervisor, either encourage or discourage their interdependence? How could you encourage it more strongly?

2. For any of your direct reports *who manage other managers,* in what ways do they encourage interdependence among the members of their own teams? How might you help them to improve this practice? Are you accidentally (or intentionally) doing anything to discourage it?

3. In what ways are you interdependent with your peers in collaborating to achieve *your manager's* output? In what ways do you and your peers recognize and act on that interdependence? In what ways does your manager encourage or discourage it?

# Continuous Lateral Development

The final Core Component of Linked Teams is Continuous Lateral Development. In some ways, this is the hidden gem of the Iterative organization.

It's hidden because the whole thing boils down to a seemingly small instruction given by a manager to his or her team members. It's a gem because it's an instruction that creates positive effects up and down the entire organization. It even goes so far as to support succession planning and bench strength, automatically!

Before getting to what it is, let's first address the painfully obvious reason it's needed.

We've said that Alice's team is linked to the other teams, so she has to recognize that and adopt an Interdependent Approach. We've said that she has to serve as a consultative adviser to her boss, Max, and then commit to 100% Implementation of his decisions—including decisions that involve coordinating with her peers. We've said that she has to be able to make OSIR Reports recommending changes in what her peers are doing. And we've said that sometimes, when Max isn't available, Alice even has to run his meetings for him, to preserve the Consistent Meeting Rhythm.

The painfully obvious fact is that to do those things well, Alice has to have a pretty good understanding of what her peers are doing. She can't simply adopt the mentality of the traditional North American Management Model, letting others worry about their work while she worries about her own. She has to make an effort to build real knowledge of what's going on with her peers. Doing so makes her a better implementer of decisions, a better recommender to Max, a better consultative decision maker with the group, and a better coordinator between her part of the organization and the broader whole.

Max's seemingly small instruction to Alice, as soon as she joins the team, goes something like this: "Now that you've joined us, Alice, one of your first orders of business is to learn as much as you can about what your peers, Bob and Cal, are doing. To do *your own* job well, you'll need an understanding of *their* work that goes beyond the superficial. Building this understanding will make you a better consultative decision maker, a stronger contributor to Upward Looking Success, and a more effective member of our interdependent team. This isn't easy and isn't something you ever truly finish doing. I'm still working at it myself and so are Bob and Cal. To start, make a concerted effort to fully understand the Verbalized Summary Outputs and Pragmatic Dashboards being presented in our Work PreView Meetings. You can use that as the basis for your first one-on-one conversations with Bob and Cal. Please get in the habit of having those conversations. You'll need them to build rapport and to learn from each other. This learning goes both ways: Bob and Cal will want to learn from you, too. And please realize that before you got here, Bob and Cal were doing the same thing with your predecessor. So listen carefully to them in your first few meetings because there's a good chance they'll have something to teach you about your own job, too."

When Alice first joins the team, she knows little about her peers' work, but that doesn't completely stop her from operating as an Iterative manager. She can still take an Interdependent Approach, still participate in Group Decision-Making, and still work toward Upward Looking Success. But as she does so, she'll be uncomfortable; she'll keep wishing she knew more about what the others are doing.

As she follows Max's advice—meeting one-on-one with her peers and learning more about what matters in their work—she'll start to improve at her management job. She'll start making solid, useful recommendations with her OSIR Reports. And she'll come to understand her interdependence on a visceral level, because she'll have a better appreciation of *both* sides of the trade-offs she's constantly making with Bob and Cal.

And here's the best part: sooner or later, Max will move up, move over, or move out. At that moment, his team will already be populated with *three* qualified replacements for him—Alice, Bob, and Cal. They all know quite a bit about each other's work; they're already working toward Max's VSO of Orange, Black, and Green; and they've each taken turns running Max's Work PreView Meeting.

Imagine that the organization selects Alice to take Max's place. If Max used to run the company, then when Alice takes over, she reports to the board or the ownership. But if Max had a manager too—maybe he was a general manager of a division—then Alice joins *that* Linked Team—the one that used to be above her. *That* manager gives Alice the same Continuous Lateral Development pep talk that Max gave her when she started with him. And on day one of her new job, Alice's new learning curve starts over again—she starts trying to learn about the work of her *new* peers. But meanwhile, on day one *she already knows about the work of her old peers*. She's ready to run the whole Orange/Black/Green organization.

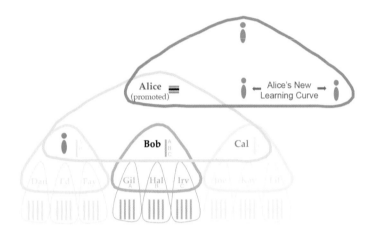

Once promoted, Alice's learning curve involves her new peers, not her old ones.

Compare this with the traditional North American Management Model—without Continuous Lateral Development. In that scenario, the whole time Alice worked for Max, she wouldn't have been worried about what Bob or Cal were doing. "That's their problem and Max's problem," she would have said to herself. Had she tried to get involved in those areas, Max, Bob, or Cal might even have discouraged it: "Your peers don't want you putting your nose in their work."

The day she got promoted into Max's job, though, she'd sure have to start worrying about Bob and Cal's work—and she'd be too late! In a high-level team, it could take her six months to a year to learn enough to run the group effectively. In the meantime, she might accidentally be inclined to either favor or micromanage the work of the person who took over her old job—since that's what she understands. This situation isn't good for the organization—and it's not good for Alice's reputation in management, either.

Continuous Lateral Development stems from a small instruction, but it has a huge impact. By constantly developing laterally, the whole organization is improving its ability to make decisions today, and it's building its talent pipeline for tomorrow. You might even say the organization is, itself, *Iterating* toward its future, more optimal state.

—————————— ACTIVITY ——————————

Reflect on the practice of Continuous Lateral Development in your organization.

1.  How well do you think your direct reports understand each other's work? What could you do to encourage more Lateral Development on your team? How equipped are your direct reports to take over your job? How could you improve this?

2.  For anyone you manage *who manages other managers,* to what extent are they encouraging Lateral Development among their own teams? One way to learn more about this is to ask about their succession plans. Who have they identified who could take their places? How might you encourage them to improve Continuous Lateral Development on their teams?

3.  How well do you understand the work of your peers? What could you do to understand it better? In what ways does your manager encourage or discourage this?

## Matrix or Cross-Functional Management

So far, we've been discussing Alice only in her direct-reporting relationship to Max. But the same principles of Upward Looking Success and Linked Teams apply to matrix or cross-functional management as well.

Here's one example: Perhaps Max has added something else to his plan, Purple. This could be the development and release of a new service. Or maybe it's overseeing a standing forum for making cross-functional resource decisions, like some kind of change control board. Whatever it is, it involves a *working group*—a cross-functional meeting that allocates resources—which Alice is heading up. You can see how the new output appears in her VSO. (Pictured at the top of page 130.)

And because it appears in Max's VSO, too, Alice can pull from anywhere in his organization to get it done. She'll be supported wherever she goes; Bob and Cal don't succeed unless Purple gets done too. So Alice runs the Purple working group as a regular Work PreView Meeting—just like her Orange ABC meeting—and she links the Purple team output to Max's higher-level team. Max, of course, owes the Purple output to the higher-level organization. Even though the membership is overlapping, Linked Teams and Upward Looking

Success still apply. In fact, all of the Key Practices discussed so far apply to Alice's management of the Purple working group and to Max's management of what is now the Orange/Black/Green/Purple team.

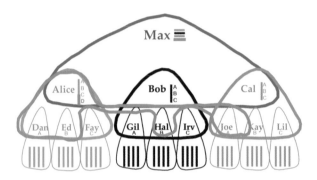

Max adds a new output resourced by his team;
Alice takes ownership and pulls resources from across the organization.

Here's a second example. What if there's a problem with Black? This impacts Max, and it's a cross-functional problem, so Bob charters a *task force*—a cross-functional team to find solutions. He's the executive sponsor. The problem seems to be with Black B, so Hal chairs the task force. Membership, again, can come from anywhere in the organization, and it can come from any level. Alice gladly joins as a *member* of Hal's team if she's needed, even though she's technically his superior; everyone's focus is on output. And like all task forces, this meeting will only last until the problem is solved. As long as it's going on, Linked Teams and Upward Looking Success apply, and Hal will run the meeting in the same way all management meetings are run.

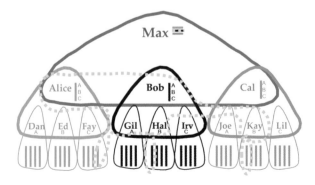

Bob sponsors a task force to solve an issue with Black; Hal chairs, and Alice is a member.

In real life, many such cross-functional teams run in parallel. If you tried to draw them all, the picture would be incomprehensible; it would look like a bowl of spaghetti. More importantly, it certainly *wouldn't* look like an organization chart. The beauty of the Iterative organization is that you don't need to diagram the whole thing, any more than you need to map your path to the car before you start crossing the parking lot. Through Linked Teams with Upward Looking Success, *the system controls itself.* Each meeting will, by definition, have a clear purpose and be kept active only as long as it's needed. And each meeting will *link* to the output goals of the larger organization. Matrix or dotted-line reporting arrangements will arise and dissolve as needed, and the organization will keep Iterating.

In the end, that's the best reason to think in terms of Linked Teams instead of organization charts; it's the only reason, really. This representation of teams is a better reflection of what's *actually going on.* People *are* crossing organizational lines. They *are* trying to figure out how to get things done. Linked Teams and the other Iterative Management practices simply provide a model that *helps* them do so instead of one that gets in their way.

## SURVIVING MANAGEMENT

Management—even Iterative Management—often feels like an endless stream of meetings and conversations, all about what's wrong and what needs to be changed. To survive it, apply these seven secrets that you won't find hidden in your company's organization chart.

*Embrace complexity.* Your work and your company's work *are* complicated—it's that simple! To get it done requires endless conversations and frequent changes. If you can come to terms with this, the work won't get any easier, but you'll be less stressed by it.

*Focus on effective meetings.* Every conversation is a meeting. If you don't get good at having clear meetings that use time wisely, you'll drown in the waste. You need to excel at having good meetings with crisp purpose statements and clear agendas.

*Build an empowering reputation.* Do you know what you're doing? Will you do what you promise? Your reputation rests on the answers your colleagues give to those questions about you. Your management role requires you to constantly influence and negotiate on behalf of your team; those negotiations will go much more smoothly if the answer to both questions is "yes."

*Reinforce common goals.* Sooner or later as a manager—probably sooner—you're going to bump into two people who have conflicting objectives. Your job is not to referee a fight but to focus everyone on the higher-level goal. Make sure you know those higher-level goals, and know how to talk about them.

*Focus on priorities.* For the rest of that conversation, keep bringing the topic back to prioritization. You're not a judge picking the better debater; you're a prioritizer of resources based on your understanding of higher-level goals. Make it clear that that's what you're doing, and do it as well as you can.

*Embody the matrix.* Before long you'll find yourself caught between conflicting priorities: two important people want two different things, and you can't do both. Under no circumstances should you promise each of them what they want, then go to your desk and cry! Instead, own the tension: communicate the "other" pressures on you to everyone. You've found a real dilemma faced by the organization, and it's your job to sort it out. Teach the organization to get smarter about the conflicts it has and how you're resolving them.

*Encourage interdependence.* Balance being assertive with being responsive. Pay attention every time to whether you should push back or concede ground. The truth is, you and everybody else in this system are interdependent on each other. There's no such thing as a win or a loss, just a decision that may change again tomorrow.

## ▶ WATCH THE VIDEO!

Your copy of this book includes prepaid access to a library of videos, including *Surviving Management*. You can watch the video now, then return to it later to refresh your memory or share concepts with others. Create your free account and watch any video, anytime, at **IterateNow.com.**

──────── ACTIVITY ────────

Reflect on Linked Teams in your organization.

1. Review the original exercise (activity #2 on page 25) where you drew your organization as Linked Teams. Make any adjustments you want to now. Try to incorporate upper and lower levels if you can.

2. Identify a few important cross-functional meetings—either working groups or task forces. Try to draw those on the same diagram. See if you can identify which manager is running the meeting and which next-level manager is owning responsibility for the outcome. Are there any meetings that seem to exist without support from the broader organization?

3. Consider any of your direct reports who run matrix, cross-functional, or similar working groups or task forces. What information about Linked Teams could you share to improve their performance and/or engagement?

## SUMMARY: LINKED TEAMS

By conceptualizing itself as a set of Linked Teams, each piece of the organization is better able to share information and make decisions as a high-functioning team *that's coordinated with other high-functioning teams.* Upward Looking Success reduces silos, putting peers in collaboration with each other. Managers as Links defines the importance of that collaboration, and Interdependent Approach acknowledges the complexity it entails. And only through Continuous Lateral Development of all managers, all the time, can the organization keep pace with its need for management development and prepare itself for sustained growth.

──────── ACTIVITY ────────

Remember, no matter how much your own organization does or doesn't formalize the concept of Linked Teams, chances are cross-functional work is going on anyway. As always, consider *labels* separately from *actual behaviors* as you work on these questions.

1. Consider any cross-functional working groups or task forces you chair. To what extent are they tied to the output of a higher-level sponsoring manager? To what extent do you run them using the Core Components presented so far, especially Upward Looking Success, Group Consultative Process, Disciplined Meeting Management, and Managers as Links?

2. To what extent do you run your own regular staff meeting as a Linked Team using those same Core Components?

3. At the end of chapter 4, you began making plans to try holding a Work PreView Meeting with your own team, using OSIR Reports. You were asked not to take any action until finishing chapters 5 and 6. At this point, now that you're clear about Group Decision-Making and Linked Teams, return to your plans. Create an agenda and hold an actual meeting with your team that is purely OSIR-driven. Have each manager on your team bring an OSIR Report for his or her most important issue, then pick one and use Group Decision-Making to discuss it in the context of your own output targets. Try to reach a clear Fully Commissioned Decision.

4. If you manage people *who manage other managers,* converse with them about how they create Upward Looking Success on their own teams. Consider whether you could help them create an OSIR-driven meeting that's focused on their own higher-level output commitment to you rather than their subordinates' output commitments to them.

CHAPTER 7

# FRONT LINE SELF-SUFFICIENCY

Simple, clear purpose and principles give rise to complex, intelligent behavior. Complex rules and regulations give rise to simple, stupid behavior.
–DEE HOCK

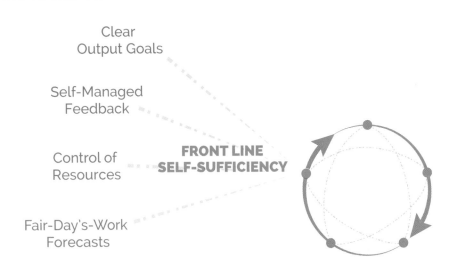

Clear
Output Goals

Self-Managed
Feedback

Control of
Resources

**FRONT LINE
SELF-SUFFICIENCY**

Fair-Day's-Work
Forecasts

Now that we've finished talking about Linked Teams, we've finished talking about how managers manage *other managers* in an Iterative organization. Max and Alice each run a Linked Team with their reports—they hold regular, forward-looking Work PreView Meetings, and in them they use good Group Decision-Making to change resource allocation as needed so that they hit the targets articulated in their Output & Status Broadcasting.

But we haven't talked about how Dan, Ed, and Fay manage their individual contributors yet. And we need to, for two reasons.

First, and most obvious, those front line employees are the ones who are producing the output of the organization. They're the ones making the products and delivering the services. If they aren't managed well, it's hard to believe we're going to have a high-performing, Iterative organization—no matter how well things seem to be going in the rest of management.

Second, and equally important, these employees know what's happening on the ground. In the analogy of walking to your car, they're your feet! In your business, they're the ones who know what's going on with the products and the customers. They have the knowledge that the rest of management needs to make good decisions.

Remember the decision made based on Alice's OSIR Report?

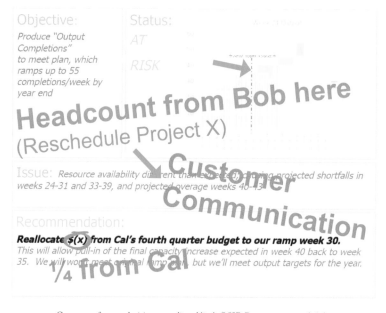

Outcome of group decision regarding Alice's OSIR Report: annotated slide.

That report, and the discussion and decision that came out of it, are predicated on two ideas: first, the idea that Alice's organization is operating with some efficiency and, second, the idea that she can forecast the future. When Alice says, "I'm going to fall short of plan during these two time periods and then get ahead in a third one," the whole team needs to believe those two ideas if they're going to have confidence that she knows what she's talking about.

Obviously, no organization is perfectly efficient, and nobody can predict the future exactly. But if Max's team doesn't have confidence that Alice's area is running pretty well and that her forecasts are fairly accurate, the whole discussion of her OSIR Report will turn into a debate over whether her organization could just "do more to catch up" and whether anyone trusts Alice's numbers anyway. That's much less useful than debating *what we should do about this new information*. It's not productive, and it certainly doesn't lead to Iteration.

The fundamental function of front line management is to prevent that from happening by making individual contributors as self-sufficient as possible—and therefore as effective as possible—both at *delivering* their output and at *forecasting* it. In doing so, the first line of management plays a unique and critical role in enabling the rest of the organization to Iterate.

We have to be especially careful here to stay focused on the function of manage*ment* at this level of the organization and not get distracted by the (admittedly important) work of manag*ing* the individual members of the workforce. Otherwise, we could spend days caught up in debates among the "how to manage people" theories of various gurus, or we could find ourselves getting overly involved with—and overly prescriptive about—the day-to-day interactions between front line supervisors and their direct reports. That's not useful.

What *is* useful is to specify, once again, *minimum requirements*: what *must* a front line supervisor put in place in order to make individual contributors as self-sufficient as possible, and therefore as effective as possible, at delivering and forecasting their own output?

The answer has three parts, which are the first three Core Components of Front Line Self-Sufficiency: **Clear Output Goals, Self-Managed Feedback,** and **Control of Resources**. These are *what* must be in place if individual contributors are going to help the organization Iterate. And they're followed by the fourth Core Component, **Fair-Day's-Work Forecasts,** which is the *why*. That's the result the organization needs, the reward for getting the first three right: good information that can flow upward.

## Clear Output Goals

As always, we'll start at the top, with the first part of the *what*: if you're going to run a fast, flexible, focused management team, all of the individual contributors who roll up into your organization must be managed to meet Clear Output Goals.

Of course, you already know that management involves setting goals. Anyone who's ever read anything about management, managing, leading, facilitating, career development, or any other professional pursuit has heard all about the importance of setting goals. Be careful—the temptation here will be to assume that you're familiar with this concept and skip over it. But that would be a bad idea, because the phrase "Clear Output Goals" has two other words besides the word "goals." And those two words make all the difference.

First, there's "clear." Individual contributors need to be working toward goals that *clearly* define exactly what they're supposed to do. Sound obvious? Well, research shows that although managers may *know* they need to set clear goals, in practice most of them aren't succeeding. The majority of goals out there seem to be, at best, less clear than they could be and, at worst, downright confusing.

Second, there's "output." The goals that are defined for individual contributors must be set in terms of *output*, not task or process. This one sounds easy too, but it's just as easy to get wrong. Front line supervisors usually know the exact tasks their individual contributors need to be performing, so the conversation naturally turns to things like taking orders or entering data. But remember the "Look, Ma!" test: order taking and data entry by themselves are tasks, or perhaps processes, but not outputs. They only become countable outputs when you start to get quite specific about details like how many, over what time frame, at what quality level, and with what result.

Clear Output Goals are a lot harder to come up with than vague task or process goals. But they make a big difference. Strangely enough, they often seem obvious—but only in retrospect.

Let me give you a personal example. I have a direct report, an individual contributor who manages my calendar. She does other things, too, but managing my calendar is one of the key functions of her position. And I used that phrase, "manage my calendar," in the written job description when we first started looking for someone to fill the position. I used it in interviews when we were screening candidates. And I used it in her training after we hired her. "Please," I said, "manage my calendar."

The problem is that "manage my calendar" is *not* a Clear Output Goal.

How is she supposed to know when my calendar is "managed"? How do I know?

So we started working on the goal. We played with ideas like response time to meeting requests. We tried to define accuracy requirements for bookings in the near future versus the distant future, and we wrangled with the importance of double bookings and how they should be handled. It wasn't easy, and it took us a few tries, but the more we focused on being *clear* and on defining *output*, the closer we got.

Here's what we finally settled on: *ensure that my calendar reflects reality*.

Thanks to this Clear Output Goal, today we both know exactly what she's supposed to produce. It passes the "Look, Ma!" test because we can both see when she gets it right. And it's measurable—all we have to do is compare what's happening in real life to what's in my calendar.

As a result, the goal has made her more self-sufficient: she no longer feels pressure to check in with me about whether to hold time for tentative items or about every double booking that comes up. If something is tentative, she marks it that way, because that's reality. If it's confirmed, she marks it that way, because that's reality. And if I'm double booked, the calendar shows it, because that's reality—and she knows she has to resolve the conflict before the day of the meetings, because I can't be in two places at once in reality. Other than needing me to make priority decisions about certain conflicts, she's now almost completely self-sufficient in managing my calendar.

Clear Output Goals are the beginning of Front Line Self-Sufficiency.

How do you create Clear Output Goals? Or, more importantly, how do you improve existing front line goals? There's not one right way. As long as you end up with a goal that's clear, accurate, and output based, you've succeeded. There are frameworks that can help. (See the sidebar on SMART Goals for one of them.) But it's equally important to realize that—as with my calendar—this is often accomplished over time, not all at once. Think of Clear Output Goals more as a continuous improvement process than as one big, goal-changing party with earth-shattering results.

# SMART GOALS

There's a game we can play called Bring Me a Rock. Here's how it goes: I say to you, "Bring me a rock," and you come back with a rock. Then I say to you, "No, I wanted a smaller rock," and you come back with a smaller rock. Once again I say to you, "No, I wanted a different color rock," and you come back with a different color rock. We can go on like this forever. Bring Me a Rock may start out funny, but it quickly becomes frustrating for everyone involved.

When you're talking about asking somebody to do something at work, playing Bring Me a Rock is not only frustrating, it's demoralizing, and it wastes time and resources. The way to avoid that is by an old trick called Setting SMART Goals. When you ask someone to do something, your request follows five criteria to be SMART.

The *S* stands for specific; the request should be tapered to a fine point. So you wouldn't tell an employee to "go find out what's going on in sales." Instead you might say, "There's been a 10% decrease in sales figures over the last six months. Please find me some root causes." That's a more specific, narrower request.

The *M* stand for measurable; that means there's a clear measuring stick—a criteria that everyone can use to determine what success looks like and when it has been achieved. Do you want three root causes for the sales decline? Do you want a report published to some forum? Do you want something implemented that will get the sales figures back up by a few percent? Those are three very different measures of success for the same specific goal.

The *A* stands for attainable—or in the most recent research, *aggressively* attainable. "Climb to the top of Mount Everest this weekend" may be specific and measurable, but it's not going to happen. Similarly, "Produce a 400% increase in company revenue" may be something your employee understands perfectly but can't possibly produce. If your request isn't attainable, there's no chance of success. And if you don't know what's attainable, you'll need to work with someone—maybe the employee him- or herself—to figure it out before you assign anything.

The *R* stands for relevant. This means that the goal relates to the existing work or expertise of the person to whom it's assigned. If you manage someone who works in IT supporting computers and you task that person with looking into sales figures, it might not seem like a relevant request—unless the problem is in the customer relationship management (CRM) or accounting software. As the one assigning the goal, you should be able to explain how it relates both to the bigger picture and to the role of the person doing it.

Finally, the *T* stands for time-bound. This simply means that every goal has a due date so that—again—everyone is clear whether or not it is reached. Do you need the root causes for the sales decline in time for the team meeting next week, or can they be delivered at the end of the month?

The next time you ask someone to do something for you at work—whether you're setting a major goal or asking for a small favor—take a few minutes to figure out the SMART criteria in advance. It will save you and the person you're working with a lot of time, energy, and frustration—and it will keep you from playing Bring Me a Rock.

### ▶ WATCH THE VIDEO!

Your copy of this book includes prepaid access to a library of videos, including **SMART Goals—Don't Bring Me a Rock**. You can watch the video now, then return to it later to refresh your memory or share concepts with others. Create your free account and watch any video, anytime, at **IterateNow.com**.

Front Line Self-Sufficiency as a whole isn't something you *finish*, any more than any other part of Iteration is ever *finished*. It's simply another part of an effort managers continually make. It's entirely possible that the Clear Output Goal for my calendar will change again. All I can tell you with certainty is that this is the best version we have *right now*. There may be a next step we can't see yet, but when we see it, we'll take it. That's what it means to Iterate.

### ACTIVITY

Reflect on the goals defined by your organization and whether they are Clear Output Goals.

1. To what extent do the individual contributors in your organization work toward goals? To what extent are those goals output oriented? To what extent are they clear?

2. Experiment with writing one Clear Output Goal. Select the work of a front line employee that you understand well, even if that person is many levels removed from you. Remember, an individual contributor will carry multiple goals. Focus on only one component of the person's work so that you can create one Clear Output Goal.

   - What is the job title or job description for that part of the work? (What would be told to a candidate for hire into the position?) Is that description output oriented, process oriented, or task oriented?

   - What is the output required from the position, as clearly as you can state it?

   - What are the quality requirements of the output? How do you tell "good" from "bad"?

   - What is the time frame for the output? List any deadline or rate requirement.

   - Summarize your answers for the previous three bullets into a statement of the goal. To what extent would that statement be understandable and memorable to the individual contributor tasked with it?

   - With whom should you discuss the goal you've just written? When?

## Self-Managed Feedback

Once an individual contributor has Clear Output Goals—a solid definition of the output he or she is supposed to deliver—the familiar question arises: So, how's it going?

That's an important one, especially in an Iterative organization. The second Core Component of Front Line Self-Sufficiency, Self-Managed Feedback, is all about making sure individual contributors have real, meaningful answers to it.

As you come across the word "feedback" yet again, remember that in this context we're talking about Front Line *Self-Sufficiency*. Traditionally, we think of it as the manager's job to give feedback to the employee. But while that can be useful and valuable, we don't want a front line that depends on the manager to figure out how things are going with their own work. That would be the opposite of self-sufficiency. Instead, we want front line employees to know *for themselves* how their work is going. Self-Managed Feedback is simply that— feedback the front line create *for themselves*.

Why is that so important?

Imagine that I'm your manager and we're in the geology business. We've agreed that your goal is to analyze twenty-five rock samples this week, each one documented in a standard form with no errors. That's a good Clear Output Goal. Now imagine that I come to you after lunch on Wednesday and tell you that we're more than halfway through the week, and you've completed only six forms—less than a quarter of the total.

How do you feel? How do you respond? Whatever you do, it will involve answering to me, your boss, about your current status. I told you *what* your status is, and now it's your job to tell me *why*.

Now, let's imagine our situation is the same, except you have Self-Managed Feedback. At the beginning of the week, you put twenty-five sticky notes on the wall, organized by day. You've been pulling down one note each time you finish processing a sample. When you get back from lunch on Wednesday afternoon, you take a look at your wall and see only six complete where there should be twelve. It's obvious that you're nowhere near halfway done; you don't need me to tell you.

How do you feel in this case? What do you do? Maybe you make a plan to catch up. Maybe *you* decide to approach *me* with some reasons for your slow progress and a warning that you might be late. But whatever you do, your answer involves taking ownership of your own work instead of waiting for your boss to tell you your own status and ask you why.

By the way, thanks to your sticky-note system, you knew a lot sooner than Wednesday afternoon that you were falling behind. You knew Tuesday morning. You probably knew by Monday afternoon. Even if I had been planning to walk in on Wednesday and ask you how it was going, long before I did, you would have been coming to me with updates and early warnings that things weren't progressing as expected.

Equipping an individual contributor to track his or her own progress—to use Self-Managed Feedback instead of relying on the manager—puts more information into the system. Raising your hand on Monday or Tuesday to say, "Hey, boss, this sample analysis isn't going as fast as I thought; I may need some help here" gives both of us a lot more time to problem-solve—to deal with the variance. In making employees more self-sufficient, Self-Managed Feedback makes them better able to identify potential future misses. That's the key to enabling the organization to Iterate—putting the front line in the driver's seat for their own work.

So, how can individual contributors track their progress with Self-Managed Feedback? Well, as you can imagine, there are many possible systems. Let me give you a few broad principles that apply, no matter the specifics.

First, *more frequent is better*. Ideally, you'd like your front line to perceive their own progress every thirty minutes—that's the frequency that we think is best matched to human neurology. But every hour is better than every two hours, every two hours is better than every day, and every day is still better than nothing.

Second, *keep it simple and visible*. In this day and age, we're tempted to computerize everything. That's not necessarily wrong. But it's a lot easier to draw a check mark on a whiteboard or pull a sticky note out of a book than it is to log into a data-tracking system and record a result—and there's a lot more open space out in real life for displaying a tracking system than there is on the screen of your favorite device.

Third, *specific feedback systems depend on Task Type*. Remember Task Type? We talked about it in conjunction with Pragmatic Dashboards: different Task Types require different forward-looking graphs. Well, no surprise, different Task Types require different Self-Managed Feedback systems, too.

Routine tasks are things like factory production and compliance approvals. The feedback systems for these are usually some form of batching, some way of making it obvious how much is done and how much remains to be done. One simple approach might be to place two boxes on your desk, an inbox filled with the work you haven't done yet and an outbox filled with the work you've completed. The sticky-note system from our geology story is another approach, letting you see what's done and what's not, in the context of how much time is left.

Troubleshooting tasks—things like technical support and disaster recovery—are different. In this case, the work isn't defined until it arrives. So Self-Managed Feedback usually takes the form of issue-status queues. Imagine you had three lists: new issues for which you don't yet know the solution, diagnosed issues where you know the solution but haven't implemented it, and completed issues where the work is done. Simply by looking at the length of each list, you'd get a sense of how your week was going and whether you were ahead or behind compared with other weeks.

Project work, the third Task Type, is different from the others. Things like construction projects or product releases have a single final output in the distant future. The only way to turn that into immediate progress is to break it down, first as sub-milestones and then as daily to-do lists. So if you owe your boss a report on Friday in support of the feasibility phase of a giant project, maybe you need a draft on Thursday, which means you need to run three tests and write two paragraphs today. That becomes your to-do list. Once you've got that written, you can see yourself making progress as you check things off.

Finally, the fourth principle: *Self-Managed Feedback is for the individual contributor only.*

This one is interesting. As your manager in our geology company, if I know you're using that sticky-note system, I may be tempted to use it too—to come by every afternoon and check how you're doing by looking at your wall. But the problem is, as soon as I do that, I've converted it from a Self-Managed Feedback system to a management information system. Now, once again, you're under pressure to either fill out your wall on schedule or explain why you haven't. The system is no longer self-managed.

There's nothing wrong with management information systems. And there's nothing wrong with the manager coming by to check in. But individual contributors need to be tracking themselves with higher frequency than the management check-ins. *They need to know how they're doing before they're asked.* They need to work at a lower level of abstraction. That way, when the manager does come by, the individual contributor tells the manager how it's going, not the other way around.

Self-Managed Feedback is used by individual contributors to do exactly that—monitor their progress in between management checkpoints. It's what lets individual contributors know how they're doing before anyone else does.

That way, when management checks in, their employees have answers. And that means information flows *upward* in the organization, not downward. When I pop into your office on Wednesday to talk about how those rock sample analyses are progressing, *you're* the one telling *me* how it's going. That's what builds trust between us. That's what sends good forecasts up the management chain from the bottom. And that's what allows the organization to Iterate.

—————————————— ACTIVITY ——————————————

Reflect on forecasts and Self-Managed Feedback in your organization.

1.  To what extent do the forecasts that come up to you from the front line and its supervisors tend to be accurate?

2.  Is the work of the individual contributors in your organization mostly routine, project based, troubleshooting, or a blend of types? If it's a blend, do you perceive that the forecasts for one type of work tend to be more or less accurate than the forecasts for another type? (For example, "Our forecasts for the routine work tend to be accurate; however, we tend to miss milestones frequently in our project work.")

3.  To what extent do you think the individual contributors in your organization are tracking their own progress outside of what management can see? To what extent do you and your management team encourage them to do so or discourage them from doing so?

4.  How might you engage front line managers and/or their individual contributors in a discussion about Self-Managed Feedback *without* giving the impression that you are installing additional management information systems or management controls?

5.  If appropriate, engage with an individual contributor to learn more about how the work is *really* tracked. Be extremely careful to avoid giving the impression that you want him or her to do anything differently. You might set it up like this: "I'm

learning about the ways in which people track their work, and your name came up as someone with a really good grasp of both your goals and your progress, so I'd like to learn more about how you do it. This is for my development, not yours, and I appreciate your time."

## Control of Resources

There's only one more requirement to make the front line as self-sufficient as possible: Control of Resources. Management is all about the allocation of resources—and if management hasn't given the front line employees ready access to the resources they need to do their jobs, those people will be inefficient instead of self-sufficient. Moreover, they'll be unable to make meaningful forecasts.

Conceptually, Control of Resources is about as obvious as it sounds: individual contributors know what resources they need, those resources are readily available, and the individual contributors can apply those resources as they see fit. *Definition*, *availability*, and *control*—that's all it takes.

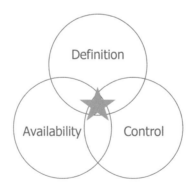

Individual contributors need definition, availability, and control of their own resources.

But be careful; this is one of those cases where the implementation can be a lot more difficult than the concept.

Imagine, for example, a fairly typical scenario in which individual contributors make requests to spend money, and someone else has to authorize the spending. So you have an employee—we'll call him Pete—whose Clear

Output Goals include timely replenishing of important supplies. In other words, people in the operation make orders to him, and he buys things each week to fill those orders—maybe light bulbs, wrenches, or laser interferometry equipment. The specifics don't matter, as long as they're well enough defined that Pete knows exactly what he's supposed to supply and how quickly.

The thing is, someone in purchasing has to approve all of Pete's planned expenditures before he can act on them. So Pete collects supply orders all week, compiles them on Friday, and then makes a budget request on Monday morning that will allow him to place the whole order.

One week Pete puts in his request on Monday morning. On Wednesday, he gets approval, and he places the order. The supplies ship by two-day air, so they're in by Friday. The following week he makes the request on Monday morning, and the approval is back by lunch, so he has the materials on site by Wednesday afternoon. The week after that, he puts the request in on Monday, but approval takes all week. He can't order until late Friday, so supplies don't arrive until after the weekend.

This makes it impossible for Pete to forecast his output. If you're his manager, your conversations go like this: "When will we have those supplies, Pete?" "Well, boss, it all depends on when I get approval." Pete will never be able to recognize whether he's ahead or behind in a given week, because he never knows what to expect.

Pete needs *definition*, *availability*, and *control* over his resources. As the manager, you start with *definition*. What is the resource Pete needs?

The easiest answer is money. How could you give Pete availability and control of the money? Can you give him a fund or budget that he controls? Can you give him automatic approval to spend under a certain limit?

Maybe you can't. Your fictitious employer has firm rules about budgets, and Pete can't be given this sort of flexibility. Don't worry; all is not lost.

A different answer to the definition question would be approvals. How could you give Pete availability and control of the approvals he needs? Can you streamline the approval process so that as long as he gets an acceptable request in by noon on Monday, he's guaranteed a response by Wednesday at ten in the morning?

If you can't do that, another answer to the definition question would be the supplies themselves. How could you make the most frequently ordered items available and give Pete control over when they get distributed? Can you give him a storeroom and allow him to carry some inventory on site, so he can fill needs immediately and then order replacements later?

Any of the solutions above would have an immediate impact, both on Pete's productivity and on his ability to tell you "how things are going." His ability to achieve his Clear Output Goals without unpredictable snags goes hand in hand with his ability to give you meaningful forecasts, including earlier warnings when things go differently than expected.

As you can see, the *definition* isn't always as straightforward as it seems. Generally speaking, resources take one of three forms: financial, as in money or budget; human, as in time or headcount; or physical, as in equipment and supplies. But within those categories you may find many options, depending on the situation and how the work is defined.

---

### ▶ WATCH THE VIDEO!

Your copy of this book includes prepaid access to a library of videos, including **Control of Resources for Individual Contributors**. You can watch the video now, then return to it later to refresh your memory or share concepts with others. Create your free account and watch any video, anytime, at **IterateNow.com**.

---

Of course, if we continued the story of Pete, it's possible that you might exhaust all of your options. Maybe there's really no way to give Pete control of a resource—any resource—that will reliably enable him to meet his Clear Output Goal of filling supply orders in a timely manner.

In that case, the conclusion wouldn't be that Pete, you as his manager, or the company that employs both of you is flawed. But it would be that Pete can't *possibly be managed well to the Clear Output Goal as it's been defined.* For whatever reasons, Pete can't be invested with the organizational resources to produce that output. Which means, if you as his front line manager can't manage him to that result, his Clear Output Goal needs to be changed.

That's not necessarily a bad thing. Maybe his measurable output should be defined as the *timely filing of approval requests.* Pete could also carry a second goal related to the *timely placing of approved orders*. That way, his job is defined as making the right requests on Monday and then acting promptly and correctly on the approvals whenever they come back. The intermediate step—the measurable output of responding to the approvals themselves—would then belong in a Clear Output Goal for a different individual managed by a different manager, probably located in the purchasing department.

In the end, either all of that would be fine or it would highlight the fact that some of the constraints on Pete's resources need to be eliminated. And that might not be easy. But nobody promised management would be easy. And fixing that problem would be an Iterative next step toward a higher-performing organization, for Pete and everyone around him.

## DEFINITION, AVAILABILITY, AND CONTROL BY TASK TYPE

When it comes to Control of Resources, it can be useful to imagine different examples of different Task Types.

For routine tasks—those involving predictable, repetitive outputs—imagine a worker in a factory, hammering nails into wooden parts in an assembly line. The Clear Output Goal could be to make a specific number of parts per hour.

- The *definition* is the list of what the worker needs to achieve that goal. The parts, the nails, and the hammer would all be included.

- *Availability* simply means making sure the factory has a sufficient supply of hammers and nails and enough raw material to keep the worker active.

- Maximizing *control* would mean making sure that, if the worker runs out of hammers, nails, or raw material, there's a place to go and get more with minimal wait.

For troubleshooting tasks—those involving solving unforeseen problems—imagine a support representative helping customers solve problems. The Clear Output Goal could be to solve a certain number of problems per time period.

- The *definition* would include whatever is needed to achieve that goal—IT equipment to communicate with customers, reference materials used to research problems, and other tools for developing solutions, even those as simple as pen and paper.

- *Availability*, again, would mean making sure that, for example, the equipment is functioning well and that the reference materials are up to date.
- Maximizing *control* would probably entail providing standard processes for resetting failed phones and computers, so that if a representative's system goes off-line, he or she can bring it back quickly and without outside help.

For project tasks—those with deliverables in the distant future—imagine the project manager of a construction project. The Clear Output Goal could be the delivery of the finished building by the deadline.

- The *definition* would include the people, budgets, and equipment to make that happen. Note that it's not enough for the performer to say, for example, "I need people." He or she must know how many, with what skills, over what time frame.
- *Availability*, once again, would involve ensuring that the organization has access to the types of equipment and people needed to complete the work.
- Maximizing *control* would require that, if the project manager needs to reassign some people to a different part of the project, he or she can do so directly, or at least without a cumbersome approval process.

---

## ACTIVITY

Consider your organization's resources and how it allows for Control of Resources by individual contributors. Remember, resources fall into one of three categories: financial, human, or physical.

1. Make a list of some of the most important resources used by the individual contributors in your organization.

2. Mark each resource as being fully in control of the individual contributor, partly in their control, or outside their control. For example, pens, pencils, and screwdrivers are fully in their control, budget may be partly in their control (within limits), and access to other employees may be outside their control.

3. For each item you marked as "partly" or "not" in their control, list the control mechanism: what's the reason or process that keeps individual contributors from controlling it fully themselves? For example, maybe the employee can't reassign heads or take budget that's not his or hers because that type of activity is reserved for managers.

4. All of these control mechanisms may seem reasonable and necessary. Even so, choose one and find a way of reducing or removing its impact. For example, you could allow a 10% budget overrun without approval but provide an incentive bonus for coming in 10% or more under budget.

5. What can the people on your management team—your direct reports and/or those lower in the organization—do to give your front line *more* Control of Resources?

## Fair-Day's-Work Forecasts

We've finished defining *what* needs to be in place for Front Line Self-Sufficiency, and we've been more than just hinting at the *why*. Before we go there, though, let's pull the first three Core Components together. Clear Output Goals ensure that the workforce knows exactly what output to deliver. Self-Managed Feedback means they know how their work is going before anyone asks. And Control of Resources means they have what they need to get the work done.

In short, individual contributors know what they're doing, they know how it's going, and they have what they need.

The result of managing the front line this way—the *why* for the Iterative organization—is our last Core Component: Fair-Day's-Work Forecasts. Individual contributors managed this way soon build an understanding of what they can reasonably accomplish in a day; they know what is a fair day's work.

Why does this happen?

First, because they *know what they're doing*. They have Clear Output Goals. They understand exactly what is expected of them and by when. The demands on them are predictable, and they feel accountability and pressure to do what they have to—today and every day—to hit those goals.

Second, they *know how it's going*. Thanks to Self-Managed Feedback, they're keeping track of their progress. And, more importantly, they've been keeping track of it for some time now; they have a base of experience to pull from. They've looked at enough inboxes to know how full is *too* full to finish in a day. They've been keeping issue queues long enough to know how many new or incomplete items at lunchtime equate to overtime this evening. They've made enough to-do lists to recognize one that will never get finished in a day.

And third, they *have what they need*. They have Control of Resources. So when they're trying to figure out how much longer it will take to do something, there's not some big caveat about how it will all depend on whether there are delays in approval signatures before shipping a package. The work is in their hands to do.

Front Line Self-Sufficiency lets individual contributors set their own daily targets within the targets set by their managers. As a result, they're both capable of hitting those targets and motivated to do so. And they're equipped to tell their managers what's *really going on* relative to those targets, because they actually know. Fair-Day's-Work Forecasts are the beginning of the good information that flows up the organization from the bottom.

## HOW MUCH SELF-SUFFICIENCY IS TOO MUCH?

One of the most common responses managers have to the idea of Front Line Self-Sufficiency is nervousness. It comes up especially strongly around Control of Resources and Fair-Day's-Work Forecasts, and it goes something like this:

"What if we put all the supplies in an unlocked location, and they get stolen?"

"What if we give people control of budgets or headcount, and they mis-manage them?"

"What if we let people predict their own timelines, and they sandbag and waste time?"

These worries and many others like them are simply various forms of doubt about trust. Sadly, this is one half of what I most commonly hear when talking with managers at all levels, in a variety of organizations: "I don't know how much I can trust the people who work for me." The other half, equally unfortunate, is: "I don't think the people who manage me are giving me *enough* trust."

Trust is a real challenge, and having an organization in which everybody feels *distrustful* of those beneath them and *distrusted* by those above them is no solution. Fortunately, the answer in both directions is the same: to build trust, both parties need to see each other *making and meeting commitments*.

Iterative Management provides a context for much of this to happen. Once everyone has Clear Output Goals (at the front line) and clear VSOs (in management), they start making commitments to each other about what they will deliver and then meeting those commitments. But that's not the whole story. Sometimes we must create additional opportunities for building trust.

This is especially true at the front line. If you're worried that employees will steal the supplies or mismanage the headcount, don't assume—exper-iment. Set a clear expectation, make a specific resource available, and monitor the results. If you're worried that front line workers will under-com-mit output, don't assume—experiment. Set some clear boundaries, trust them with some limited forecasting, and monitor the results.

By the same token, whatever level you're at, if you're worried that your manager doesn't trust you enough, don't assume—experiment. Ask directly to be trusted with *just a little more*. Agree together on some boundary con-ditions. Then help your boss monitor your results.

Experiments like these only take a little extra time, but the payoffs can be huge. Just remember, you can't create trust all at once; you have to build it one small step at a time. Don't forget to Iterate.

---
## ACTIVITY
---

Consider Fair-Day's-Work Forecasts in your organization.

1. Reflect on how well your front line employees know what they can accomplish in a given day and the extent to which you're able to know the answer to this question.

2. To what extent do individual contributors carry *separate* understandings of "what management expects me to accomplish" and "what I can actually accomplish"? How could those two realities become better aligned?

3. To what extent do front line workers share their Fair-Day's-Work Forecasts with management? Are they encouraged to share potential variance in output or penalized for doing so? How can you more strongly encourage accurate information to flow upward?

## Management and the Front Line

Before we began this chapter about Front Line Self-Sufficiency, we talked about four other Key Practices of the Iterative organization—Output & Status Broadcasting, Work PreView Meetings, Group Decision-Making, and Linked Teams. And you saw how those four practices, used together, are the best approach to managing other managers; how they get managers, metaphorically, to *look up*—both to take ownership of their own work and to see how it fits into the bigger picture.

Now, you can see that this fifth Key Practice, Front Line Self-Sufficiency, provides an equally good formula for front line managers to manage individual contributors. This is what gets front line employees to *look up*, proactively bringing changes and variances to their management's attention instead of waiting to be asked.

Let's go back to Max's organization. When Alice made an OSIR Report requesting budget dollars to get back on track, the team decided they would also transfer some employees from Bob to Alice. Now that has to happen. So Bob will take the decision to *his* Linked Team to decide who to transfer. And Alice will take the decision to *her* Linked Team to decide where to put them. There may be some special meetings between the two groups to figure everything out. And maybe, in the end, it's decided that Gil and Irv will each transfer one person to Fay, at the same time, for six months.

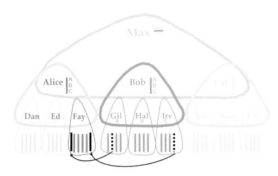

Two employees transferred to Fay's group.

So Fay, a front line manager, gains two new employees who are supposed to help her fix a problem with the production schedule. For this to work, she's got to get them up to speed quickly. What does she do?

She focuses on Front Line Self-Sufficiency. First, she takes time to ensure they *know what they're doing*—she creates and communicates Clear Output Goals. Second, she makes them understand that they *themselves* need to *know how it's going*—that's Self-Managed Feedback. She doesn't create and monitor tracking systems for them, but she does set an expectation that they will have them. She might also provide some templates or point them toward their colleagues who have good Self-Managed Feedback. Third, she makes sure they *have what they need*; she works to give them as much Control of Resources as her organization will allow.

---

▶ **WATCH THE VIDEO!**

Your copy of this book includes prepaid access to a library of videos, including *Improving Front Line Self-Sufficiency*. You can watch the video now, then return to it later to refresh your memory or share concepts with others. Create your free account and watch any video, anytime, at **IterateNow.com**.

---

Before long, Fay starts asking her new employees to *predict* their own output—to start making their Fair-Day's-Work Forecasts. She asks, "How much do you think you can get done today? How about this week? What's reasonable?" She starts checking on the extent to which they understand what's possible and asks them to notice how often they accomplish it. She knows they won't be very accurate at first, but she wants them to get into the habit of forecasting—she wants them to adopt a Forward Looking Orientation. Because the sooner they start, the sooner they *will* get good at it. And she wants them good at it. She wants them *looking up*, like everyone else on her team.

Notice how different this is from the standard North American Management Model—the one where the manager tries to check in on the employee's progress often enough to avoid every possible misstep or surprise.

In that approach we assume that the manager knows best, and knows exactly what is possible, and that it's that person's job to push, force, or drag each employee along the path to greatness. But dragging people to greatness isn't a good strategy with most human beings.

If you're trying to create engagement and retention, your odds of success are a lot better if you ask people to meet challenges that are appropriate to their skill level. The balance is tricky: if they're over-challenged, they get stressed, and if they're under-challenged, they get bored. Since only the employee truly knows where the balance point is, why not give that employee some latitude in finding it?

This is not to say that Fay shouldn't develop an opinion about the performance of her employees. Of course she should. And she's not excused from knowing what's going on with her team or from holding her employees accountable.

It's just that Fay knows what all managers know in Iterative organizations: *it's neither possible nor desirable to replace the individual contributor's initiative with her own.* Her oversight can never take the place of the intelligence and goodwill of the person doing the job today. So her job is to create a scenario that draws out their own intelligence and goodwill, rather than trying to force hers on them.

Besides, Fay has four other people to manage. And she's busy collaborating with Dan and Ed to achieve Alice's VSO. Following her two newest employees around and micromanaging them would be a poor use of her time, and it would put some of her other important output—her organization's important output—at risk.

Obviously, in the course of manag*ing* her new employees, Fay will have lots of other things to do, too—administrative and relational tasks that go beyond the three bullets of Clear Output Goals, Self-Managed Feedback, and Control of Resources. But in her manage*ment* role in Max's Iterative organization, those are her priorities and the expectation set by management above her, up to and including Max: "We strive to make our front line employees as self-sufficient as possible." If Fay gets Front Line Self-Sufficiency right, her new employees will soon know best when it comes to the real output of her organization. And that's good because they need to know best—they're the ones creating it.

---

## ACTIVITY

Consider what happens in your organization when a front line manager gets a new employee.

1. What is the process? Is there a new-hire checklist or program to assist the manager in integrating new employees?

   - If so, to what extent is that checklist or program consistent with the elements of Front Line Self-Sufficiency, including Clear Output Goals, Self-Managed Feedback, and Control of Resources? What's missing?

   - If not, to what extent do you think front line managers succeed at creating Front Line Self-Sufficiency for newly acquired employees?

2. How might this be improved?

## SUMMARY: FRONT LINE SELF-SUFFICIENCY

Front Line Self-Sufficiency enables information to flow up from those doing the work to those managing it. Clear Output Goals ensure individual contributors know exactly what they're supposed to accomplish, Self-Managed Feedback allows them to develop their own understanding of their progress, and Control of Resources eliminates any unpredictable snags. As a result, front line employees can make Fair-Day's-Work Forecasts, and management can roll up those forecasts into a clear picture of what's going to happen in the future.

———————— ACTIVITY ————————

Reflect on Front Line Self-Sufficiency in your organization.

1. To what extent do you work to make your organization's front line as self-sufficient as possible? How could you do more?

2. Which of the first four Key Practices—Output & Status Broadcasting, Work PreView Meetings, Group Decision-Making, or Linked Teams—would be most helpful in increasing the self-sufficiency of the *managers* who report in to you directly? How about the managers who roll up to you via other managers?

3. Which aspect of Front Line Self-Sufficiency—Clear Output Goals, Self-Managed Feedback, or Control of Resources— would be most helpful in increasing the self-sufficiency of the *individual contributors* who roll up to you?

4. In what way does your own manager work to make you more self-sufficient? In what way does he or she hinder your self-sufficiency? Which of the Five Key Management Practices would help? What could you ask for?

# CHAPTER 8

# UNDERSTAND, ASSESS, AND IMPROVE

The only thing of real importance that leaders do is to create
and manage culture.
–EDGAR SCHEIN

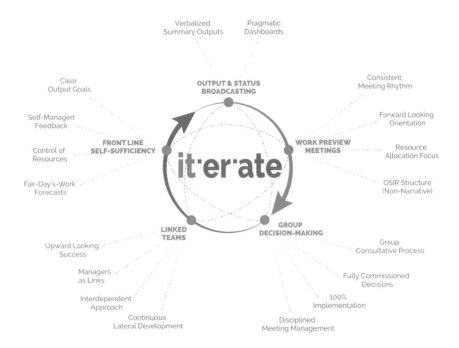

We started this book with three goals: to *understand* what managers do in high-performing, Iterative organizations; to *assess* the extent to which you and the other managers in your organization do those things; and to *improve* your own organization by increasing some of those behaviors, even by a little. Could you possibly run your organization a bit more like Max runs his?

Well, we've finished with *understand*: we've stepped through the Five Key Practices and eighteen Core Components, which fully define what management should be doing in order to serve as the organization's feedback system. We've explored Max's organization thoroughly and looked at his team as a clear example of Iterative Management in action. And we've tried to remind ourselves that Iterative Management is all about behavior, not labels—about *what people are doing*, not *what we call it*. Take a moment now to review appendix 5—it's a full description of Iterative Management that you can use to run your own management team, even though it never mentions anything about Key Practices or Core Components.

---

▶ **WATCH THE VIDEO!**

Your copy of this book includes prepaid access to a library of videos. Now that you've been introduced to the Five Key Practices, take one last look at Alice, with additional commentary, in ***The Story of Alice—Observing an Organization***. You can watch the video now, then return to it later to refresh your memory or share concepts with others. Create your free account and watch any video, anytime, at **IterateNow.com**.

---

## From Understand to Assess

Along the way, you've been working on *assess* and even *improve*, too. You've taken the time to observe your own organization, you've reflected on how it compares to Alice's, and you've even tried some different behaviors with your own direct reports and coworkers.

Now you're going to finish with *assess*. You're about to look over your notes one last time to compare what you see around you to what you learned from Max's management of Alice. Then, you'll complete the "Assessment of Iterative Management Practices," if you haven't already done so, and you'll take a final, serious look at where your own biggest opportunities lie. Once that's done, you'll be ready to finalize your plan to *improve*.

But before you do any of that, we need to check in about three things.

First, remember that *understand comes before assess*. If you don't feel as if you fully comprehend any of the Five Key Practices or eighteen Core Components, now is the time to go back and review whatever you need. Get yourself as clear as can be about the practices, how they work, and how they relate to each other. The clearer your understanding is, the better your assessment will be.

Second, *Iteration isn't exciting or glamorous*. At the beginning of chapter 1, I said that the walk to your car is probably the least interesting, least memorable part of your day. The same is true about Iterative Management—the set of behaviors that allow all members of management to work together as the feedback system. It's just not sexy, not like some of the other things you do as a manager. It's true: things like *getting clear about our values* or *working on a new strategy* or even *redoubling our efforts* have a certain attractiveness to them. They can be exciting! And so can some of the things you do in the course of mana*ging* individuals—like helping an employee deal with a difficult situation or encouraging someone's career development.

Those things are also important. Deciding who you are as an organization, deciding what you want to accomplish, and committing to work hard to get there are critical. So are helping employees and supporting their development. But if you don't *also* attend to the mechanics that make everything happen—the operation of manage*ment* and the specifics of how it *enables* your organization to be what it wants to be and get where it wants to go—you're missing something that can't be replaced. Iteration isn't sexy, but it's no less important.

---

## FOUR HORRIBLE TRUTHS
## OF MANAGEMENT

We've covered these throughout the book. Now, review them one more time, take a deep breath, and commit to your role in management anyway. What you do is vital to your organization. Besides, no job is perfect, right?

**Management isn't sexy.** Making incremental adjustments to organizational resources to keep the enterprise on target may be the least attractive part of the work, as viewed from the outside. It's not high-tech, it's not customer facing, and it's not terribly exciting to talk about. The fact that acting as the feedback system for the organization is critically important—and that it can be interesting and engaging to the manager who's actually *doing it*—doesn't change any of that.

**Management is about being "wrong."** In Iteration, every step leads to new information, and every new piece of information informs every step. Management is about making the best decision possible and then discovering upon implementation that things aren't going as planned. Often that discovery comes packaged as criticism: "Why didn't you see this coming?" The truth is, often management *can't* see it coming. All it can do—must do—is adjust and adjust again. Fail forward, fast.

**Management can only allocate resources.** The management team can't change the customer, the products, the services, the marketplace, the board, the ownership, or the future. All it can do is assign resources—people, money, and equipment—to get the work done. And since most resources are fully assigned, all it can really do is contemplate *changes* to resource assignments already in place. The only decision management ever makes is whether to leave resources alone or, if not, how to move them around.

**Management is succeeding when it's resource constrained.** Moving resources around almost always involves taking them *away from* something else. That's because the balance between opportunities and resources is never perfect, and it's preferable to have too few resources rather than too few opportunities. In the best-case scenario, management is all about stealing resources from *good* opportunities to apply them to *better* ones. And while that sounds good on paper, in reality it makes for some terribly difficult decisions, especially since those not-good-enough options always have strong, emotional advocates.

## ▶ WATCH THE VIDEO!

Your copy of this book includes prepaid access to a library of videos, including *Four Horrible Truths of Management*. You can watch the video now, then return to it later to refresh your memory or share concepts with others. Create your free account and watch any video, anytime, at **IterateNow.com**.

Actually, the more routine and predictable management gets, the better. Think about this: the fact that you have automatic, invisible, relatively boring systematic behavior helping you walk to your car on time is what frees up your higher-level thinking for looking further forward. What route will you take once you're in the car? What will you order for dinner? What's your schedule like tomorrow? You couldn't work on any of those things if you were too preoccupied with the walk. And it would do you little good to arrive on time to your car only to find you hadn't devoted any cognitive resources to what you would do after you got there. It's exactly the same in organizations. You need your management to Iterate—systematically and *automatically*—so that higher-level attention can be focused further out on the marketplace, on the next generation, on the competition.

When you're working on Iterative Management, don't mix up "sexiness" with importance. Be secure in the knowledge that you're working on something critical, and don't allow yourself to get distracted by its more exciting relatives, like strategy, values, hard work, and the requirements of managing individuals. They're all parts of the same whole.

Third, and finally, *as you assess, prepare to face the temptation to surrender.* That's the temptation to say, "This all sounds good, but there's nothing *I* can do about it." You may have felt the temptation already, and if you did, thanks for sticking around. That feeling is only going to get stronger now. As you get ready to move into *assess* and *improve*—as you get more specific about what you might want to change—you're going to encounter internal resistance. Because there's a part of you—a part of all of us—that doesn't like change. And that part is going to say some things that sound like this: "Oh, sure, it works for Max because he manages Alice in a fake organization. I live in the real world."

Or "I'm just one person. I don't have the power to change everything."

Or how about this one: "Ed Muzio doesn't have any idea of the unique problems and difficulties I face in my job."

Let's not argue with any of those. In fact, let's just agree to all of them. Max's organization is, in fact, an oversimplified cartoon. Real life is much messier. You are, in fact, one person. I counted! And I, Ed Muzio, don't know what's going on in your job. Seriously, I can't even *see* you!

And doesn't that make you wonder, just a little, *how* I counted?

Yes, I'm being a little silly here, for a reason. When you start creating stories about how this or that will never work or about how your challenges are *so* uniquely difficult as to be unsolvable, you start building thought barriers that prevent the kind of flexible thinking you need to effect change in a complex system. On the other hand, when you lighten up, use humor, and start thinking and speaking more openly and positively about ideas, possibilities, and opportunities, you open up thinking modes that allow you to create solutions. In short, joking around, staying open, being playful, and considering crazy ideas all activate your brain—at least, the part of it you need to do this kind of thing.

You *will* face the temptation to surrender. When you do, try to answer it that way. Laugh at it. Tell it that you haven't found the answer—yet. Or remind it that people less smart than you have solved problems like these before.

You are not the first person to manage a group of humans who are trying to do something complicated or something nobody has done before. You're not the first person to face unusual challenges, time pressure, and resource constraints. You're not the first person with—you know—a *boss*. Don't let the part of you that doesn't like change talk the rest of you into believing that change isn't possible. Because you won't be the first person who ever made a positive impact despite a healthy dose of skepticism, either.

---

## ASSESS NOW!

Your copy of this book includes one prepaid license to take the "Assessment of Iterative Management Practices." Your instant, customized report describes how effectively both you and your manager use the Five Key Practices, and it helps you identify potential improvements. Create your free account and access your assessment at **IterateNow.com**.

---

## ACTIVITY

Expand on your assessment of your own organization's Iterative Management.

1. Look over all of your notes, especially those from the Summary sections of chapters 3 through 7. Which of the Five Key Practices and eighteen Core Components did you note as being present in your organization? Which did you note as missing?

2. If you haven't already, take the "Assessment of Iterative Management Practices." Review your results; compare and contrast them with your notes from question 1 above.

3. Return to your notes from The Story of Alice in chapter 2. Consider again the similarities and differences between Alice's organization and the one you run.

4. Look at the *Iterate* graphic at the start of this chapter showing the Five Key Practices and eighteen Core Components. Based on your analysis above and your notes and reflections in the previous activity, mark one to three items that are *most like* the organization you run—which are its strengths—and one to three items that are *least like* it—which are its opportunities. Then, identify the *one area* you'd most like to improve first, and write down some potential first steps. Stay focused on the part of the organization that *you* run.

5. After you make your plan, look once again at the results of your "Assessment of Iterative Management Practices." Pay special attention to the *differences* between how you scored yourself and how you scored your manager on your area of focus.

   - If you are choosing to improve an area in which you scored your manager as *weaker than you,* it means that you are choosing to model something different than what your team sees from the rest of your organization.

   - If you are choosing to improve an area in which you scored your manager as *stronger than you,* it means you can rely on your manager as a model and perhaps a resource as you attempt to improve your own organization.

- Either is fine, as long as you're aware of the dynamic between you and your manager. And either way, be limited and specific in identifying your first steps. It's better to succeed at a modest commitment than to fail at a larger one!

## From Assess to Improve

You're about to complete this book. Congratulations! You've noticed the strengths of your own organization—the ways in which it does Iterate. And you've identified some opportunities for improvement—areas where your workplace seems least Iterative, areas that need the most help.

Those weaknesses are exactly what you need to know because of the nature of the Five Key Practices. Remember how, when we started, I pointed out the connecting lines between each of the Key Practices? They're there to remind us that the practices are interdependent—they work together as a system. Each one depends on all of the others.

For example, Work PreView Meetings get better when Output & Status Broadcasting gets better, because the OSIR Reports are clearer. Work PreView Meetings get better when Front Line Self-Sufficiency gets better, because the forecasts get better. Work PreView Meetings get better when Linked Teams get better, because the decisions benefit the broader organization. And Work PreView Meetings get better when Group Decision-Making gets better, because the decisions made are higher quality.

Or we can start somewhere else. Group Decision-Making gets better when Work PreView Meetings get better, because the group is set up with clear OSIR Reports to make the right decisions. Group Decision-Making gets better when Output & Status Broadcasting gets better, because each team member can more clearly explain impacts to their work. Group Decision-Making gets better when . . . well, you get the idea.

That's why the *assess* step is so important; each Key Practice is supported by all the others. If you find and improve the weakest one, *you improve them all.* Even your organization's strengths get stronger when you address your weaknesses.

So, what can *you* do about your weaknesses?

If you're like a lot of people, this is where your *temptation to surrender* will be strongest. After all, we're talking about systematic behaviors across all the people around you. What can *you* possibly do to change things? We're asking you to do nothing less than improve the management culture in your organization, at least a little.

But what can one person do to improve the culture?

Fortunately, there's an answer to that question. We tend to think of culture as being a sort of ether around the organization—an invisible fog that affects us from outside of our control, like the weather. Culture impacts customer satisfaction, output and quality, employee retention, employee engagement—almost everything! But while it's easy to think of *it* acting on *us*, it's a lot harder to think about how *we* act on *it*. The truth is, you can, should, and do act on your organization's culture—whether you know it or not.

To talk about this, we need to be clear about the definition of organizational culture. I prefer to use the definition from Edgar Schein of MIT Sloan, who we think invented the term: "The culture of a group can now be defined as: A pattern of shared basic assumptions that the group learned as it solved its problems of external adaptation and internal integration, that has worked well enough to be considered valid and therefore, to be taught to new members as the correct way to perceive, think, and feel in relation to those problems."

In other words, the people of the past had some problems and evolved some behaviors to solve those problems, which we now model to each other, often unconsciously, in the present way we do things. And that's the culture.

This definition has an important implication: the behaviors of the present—at least some of them—will also carry forward into the future. So the question is, *which* present behaviors—that is, *which of your behaviors*—will turn into the future culture?

Consider four factors that can make one of your behaviors *today* turn into the culture of *tomorrow*: First, what you're doing has to be *ascensive*. It has to be helpful—to make things go up or get better—because if it's not a solution to anything, nobody will carry it forward. Second, it has to be *visible*, because if people can't see you doing it, they can't adopt it. Third, it has to be *duplicable*—people need to be able to copy you—so that it can be widely adopted. And finally, it has to be *feasible* for people to adopt it. It can't be too difficult for them, and it can't get them into trouble; otherwise, they won't do it.

When those four intersect—when you start doing something that's ascensive, visible, duplicable, and feasible—you've created a culture-changing behavior. People will adopt it from you without even realizing it. And you'll be changing the culture of tomorrow, right now.

All you have to do is ask yourself two questions: First, what change is needed right now? And second, what culture-changing behavior could you be doing that would help?

---

## CHANGING MEETINGS BY
## CHANGING CULTURE: AN EXAMPLE

Imagine that you manage an organization that holds a lot of disorganized meetings—people getting together without clear agendas or disciplined structure. In reading about Disciplined Meeting Management, you decide that better agendas would help your own meetings. But you want to go further—you want to improve your part of the organization. So you've decided that your *use of clear meeting agendas* should be a culture-changing behavior. To succeed, your use of agendas will have to meet the four criteria for culture-changing behaviors.

First, it must be *ascensive*—it has to make things better! If you start creating and reading out verbose, complex agendas in your meetings and, in doing so, make them longer or overly restrictive, you'll make little progress in creating culture change. On the other hand, if your new use of agendas makes your meetings shorter or more relevant or more accessible for people wanting to raise real concerns, that's ascensive—that gives people good reason to consider trying your behavior for themselves.

Second, your new behavior has to be *visible*. If your agendas exist only in your mind, they might guide your thoughts as you run your meetings, but that behavior will be invisible to everyone else. Nobody can adopt behavior they can't recognize. On the other hand, if you put what you're doing on display in each meeting—"I've found it useful to use agendas, so here's the one I've created"—you will have created a visible behavior. And people who can see what you're doing have the option to try it themselves.

That leads to number three: your use of agendas has to be *duplicable*. That means other people must be in a position to make use of it. If your meetings are populated by individual contributors who don't run meetings themselves, it won't matter how much they *like* your behavior, because they'll have no context in which to duplicate it. But if the attendees in your meetings are managers with meetings of their own to run, your behavior becomes duplicable, because it will be applicable to their circumstances as well as yours.

Finally, your new behavior must be *feasible*; the people around you must *be able* to duplicate it, if they want to try. They need the *knowledge, skills, and abilities* to do it themselves. They must either know how or learn how to write good agendas. Equally importantly, they need *social permission* to do it. They must believe that if they start using better agendas, their bosses won't fire them, their employees won't quit, and their spouses won't leave them.

You can't control all of these issues—especially spouses!—but you can influence many of them. You can ensure that your use of agendas is productive. You can be extra articulate in describing what you're doing. You can practice your new behavior with people who can use it themselves. And you can even provide job aids and rewards to help others get started— especially since you're the boss! It won't be immediate, and it won't be perfect, but if you succeed in making your new behavior ascensive, visible, duplicable, and feasible, you will have begun to change the culture.

## ▶ WATCH THE VIDEO!

Your copy of this book includes prepaid access to a library of videos, including **Changing Culture**. You can watch the video now, then return to it later to refresh your memory or share concepts with others. Create your free account and watch any video, anytime, at **IterateNow.com**.

Don't be fooled! As you walk across the parking lot to your car, if your brain is the CEO, your cardiovascular system is middle management, and your feet are the front line, the metaphor for "organizational culture" is absolutely *not* the weather, acting on you outside your control and from a distance. A better analogy for it would be *your habits*—the way you swing your arms when you walk, whether you're smoking a cigarette, etc. It's the collection of patterns of behavior that you're used to doing and that you do *automatically*. This collection acts on you because you're habituated to it, but *you also act on it*. You can change a habit if you want to!

In the same way you or I might have good or bad habits, an organization can have productive or unproductive culture. And just as you or I could use specific tools to work on changing our own habits, now you have a framework for changing the management culture in your part of the organization:

- First, use this book to decide what needs changing. Look at the Five Key Practices and the eighteen Core Components, and decide which one of them would be most useful to the management team you run if it were improved—even a little.

- Then, do something that is ascensive, visible, duplicable, and feasible. You'll probably start with the team you manage directly (or a team you advise, if you're in an HR capacity). Take an action that helps, that those around you can see, and that those around you can copy.

That's it. Just one action. As soon as you do it, you're underway.

Know, too, that getting underway won't feel like much at first. This isn't an approach that leads to a giant overnight change in one step. But then, no approach to improving culture leads to a giant overnight change in one step.

I'm speaking from personal experience here: we have a variety of approaches to helping organizations become more Iterative—online training, simulations and workshops, even cutting-edge group interventions involving live working sessions with the head of the organzation plus two layers of management, all at once. They're all targeted at exactly the type of culture change we're talking about here, they're all designed to create improvement as quickly as possible, and they're all successful in our market because they produce real improvements quickly. And yet, they all have one thing in common: they're not instant.

Even when the president, CEO, or owner of the company opens a session with the entire management team by announcing that the company is to be different, *starting right now*—even when everyone in that room *wants* it to be different, *starting right now*—the company does not change at that moment.

Culture change is *always* a gradual, local process. There are tricks to speeding it up and mistakes that slow it down, but "instant" is never an option.

The good news is that improvement *can* start with you. Actually, since you're a manager of managers, I might even argue that it *should* start with you. You understand what it means to Iterate, you're better positioned than anyone to improve your part of the organization, and you're in the perfect position to both require and model changes on your team. And since you link your part of the organization to the whole, you might even be able to do some role modeling with your peers and boss, too.

There's more good news: you know exactly where to start. Thanks to the work you did in this book to *understand* and *assess*, you've identified which of the Iterative Management practices need the most help. You know exactly what to *improve*—what will make your own management team a little more fast, flexible, and focused. All you have to do now is choose an action—a small action, something you can do immediately. An action that's *ascensive, visible, duplicable,* and *feasible*. And then go and do it.

This is the last chapter. There's nothing more to say. It's time to turn everything over to you. You're the one running your management team. I can't encourage you strongly enough to take action here. Make a change within your own management meeting. Clarify expectations on how your team members are to run their own meetings. Make an improvement to an individual contributor's goals. Model a new kind of reporting or suggest a new kind of meeting structure to anyone who will notice.

Make a choice. Define an action. *Do something.* It's in *your* hands now.

As soon as you do, be sure to congratulate yourself, because you'll have taken the first step. And before long you'll start to see whether that step was useful or not. You'll either get more fast, flexible, and focused or you won't. And either is fine because either result is informative. Either result sets you up to take the *next* most logical step—to determine the *next* action you can take that's likely to help—the *next* thing you can do that's ascensive, visible, duplicable, and feasible. And then you can do *that*, learn from it, and repeat.

It's true: you're never going to get your culture from where it is now to where you want it to be in a single step.

But that's ok.

You can Iterate.

# APPENDIX 1

## COUNTING OUTPUT: TASK TYPE

All workplace tasks fall into one of three categories, or Task Types: routine work, troubleshooting work, or project work. The differences among them are based upon two simple characteristics of the task: *predictability*, whether the person doing the work can anticipate what it will be, and *delay tolerance*, whether it must be completed immediately or can be done later.

When predictability is high and delay tolerance is low, we call this *routine* work. Examples include things like factory production and the processing of regular compliance paperwork for approval. The people doing this kind of work know what it will be before they start. They must maintain some sort of pace to keep the outputs on schedule, but the outputs themselves don't change much. Counting "Look, Ma" outputs of this type is usually no more involved than simply tallying the completion of each unit of output.

When foresight into the output goes away—when predictability becomes low and delay tolerance is low as well—we call it *troubleshooting* work. Technical support and disaster recovery are two examples of these tasks, which must be done quickly even though they're difficult to anticipate. Until a phone call or email comes in with a problem, the performers of troubleshooting tasks don't know what to expect; once the problem arrives, they need move quickly to solve it. Quantifying this type of "Look, Ma" output generally involves some countable feature of the population of issues in queue—perhaps how many problems remain to be solved or how quickly they're being handled.

When delay tolerance moves from low to high—when people have more and more time to complete the work assigned—predictability becomes less important because there's more time to accommodate surprises and changes. This third category is what we call *project* work. Examples include construction projects and product releases. Project work has milestones and deliverables far in the future, and workers plan their tasks and manage themselves, at least to some extent, on the way to those outputs. The countable "Look, Ma" outputs here usually include both the final outcome and a set of subordinate outputs or deliverables critical to achieving it.

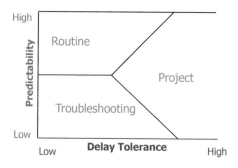

Three types of task.

Understanding the Task Type behind a given output requirement is critical, because it informs how management can count, chart, and forecast the output as well as how individual contributors can create Self-Managed Feedback for it:

- For routine tasks, individual contributors can count actual outputs and visually represent how many are done and how many remain to be done.

- For troubleshooting tasks, individual contributors can use issue-status queues to meaningfully group outputs and visually represent relative queue sizes.

- For project tasks, individual contributors can create daily to-do lists based upon their most pressing outputs in the near future and mark completion of those items.

# APPENDIX 2

## COUNTING OUTPUT: ROUTINE EXAMPLES

Often the easiest Task Type to conceptualize is routine—tasks with high predictability and low delay tolerance, like factory production or compliance approvals. One example of a routine task is Alice's VSO item B: *Produce output completions to meet plan, which ramps up to 55 completions per week by year end.* Alice's group is producing the same kind of thing week after week. They're increasing the pace throughout the year, but they know weeks and even months in advance what the output will look like.

The graph Alice uses in the example throughout the book is one example of a Really Useful Data display for routine task output.

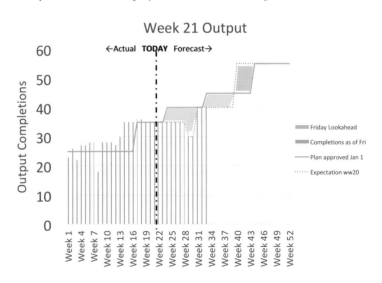

Here Alice shows three things: the orange line shows her original plan, which is her previous expectation; the blue bars show her past production relative to that target; and the orange bars and blue dotted line together display her future forecast, which is her new expectation. By shading the areas in which her new understanding of the future differs from her original plan, Alice creates a graphical lead-in to the conversation that's most needed: the one about future variance.

Of course, factory production isn't the only routine output. The second example of a way to count routine outputs involves a process where we count the number of times we've made an offer and the number of times our offer has been accepted. Volume sales, employee recruiting, and fund-raising activities all follow this kind of sequence.

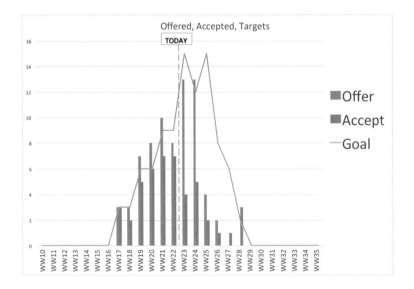

In this graph, we're showing performance of a planned campaign—an intense period of making offers with a certain response target—though the format would also apply to a more steady-state situation. The green line shows the weekly acceptance goal, the blue bars count offers made, and the red bars indicate offers accepted. When a red bar meets the green line, it indicates that the target was met in that week. Looking back, we missed our target a few times and didn't ever exceed it. And looking forward, if we don't extend a lot more offers, it's unlikely that we'll recover.

Absent the graph, in a conversation about this work, it would be easy and maybe even natural to emphasize how many offers we have out for response in the next couple weeks—weeks 23 and 24. It's a record! This might paint an optimistic picture. But the graph tells the real story: our current performance isn't going to produce the result we'd planned. What are we going to do about this? The fact that this graph raises that question so clearly is what makes it Really Useful Data.

Both of the graphs presented here provide different views of routine work, but both provide answers to the most important question for Really Useful Data: how is it going to go differently than we expected? Obviously, there are many other options, too, but hopefully this gives you a starting point to think about the display of your own routine tasks.

# APPENDIX 3

## COUNTING OUTPUT: TROUBLESHOOTING EXAMPLES

Troubleshooting tasks are defined by both predictability and delay tolerance being low—tasks like technical support and disaster recovery. This appendix contains two examples of graphs tracking this kind of work.

The first one may be appropriate for any troubleshooting situation where there's a commitment of maximum resolution time on issues customers bring.

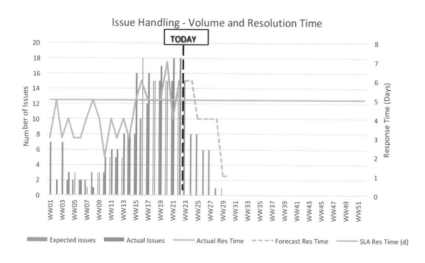

Issue Handling - Volume and Resolution Time

In this case, we have a committed response time, or Service Level Agreement (SLA), of just over five days. That's the blue line. Our actual response time is shown by the green line. We started the year well under our SLA target, but in recent weeks we've averaged up to nearly eighteen days to resolve issues. Now look at the bars. As you can see, we had several weeks where the actual number of issues received—the red—was substantially higher than what we expected—the blue. But our forecast suggests this problem is already resolving itself and the number of issues will drop substantially in the next few weeks, as will the response time. If we were simply talking about "how things are going," we might tend to focus on the fact that we've been running too long on responses. Management might be tempted to assign extra resources to combat this problem. But the graph shows the truth: if our forecasts are right, the problem is going away. Those resources are better spent elsewhere (perhaps apologizing to the customers we've already mishandled).

A different way to quantify work based on troubleshooting tasks is to count aging issues. In this case output targets are defined not in terms of how quickly each issue is resolved but in terms of how many issues of what age are still open. This approach works well for collection of overdue accounts receivable and a variety of problem-resolution scenarios ranging from IT to health care to investigative work by law enforcement. Here's a technical example in which we've separated our issues by category and expressed both a target and an actual count of issues sorted over a variety of time frames.

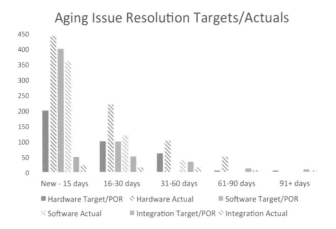

Let's look first at 16–30 days and focus first on the red bars. We expected that in the course of normal operations, we would have one hundred hardware issues of this age in the queue—that's the solid red bar. But look at the striped red bar. We *actually* have more than twice our target in queue right now. This appears to be an issue for hardware only; in comparing the striped versus solid bars that are green and blue, we can see that the actual counts of our software and integration issues for the same time horizon are much closer to our expectation.

Hardware is the major variance here. In almost every time frame, you can see that we've got more hardware issues in queue than our target. And it's most severe with the newest issues—new to 15 days—so the situation is probably getting worse instead of going away. It's worth having a management conversation about how to handle this, and the Really Useful graph makes the need for that conversation apparent.

These two graphs of troubleshooting work output are different from each other, but both answer the important question: how's it going to go differently than we expected? Obviously there are many other options, too, but hopefully this starts you thinking about how to count your own troubleshooting outputs.

# APPENDIX 4

## COUNTING OUTPUT: PROJECT EXAMPLES

Project work is defined by having high delay tolerance—examples include construction projects and product releases. This doesn't require much explanation because most organizations have at least a few projects going on, if not a few thousand. But please set aside your preconceived ideas about project management terminology as you review this appendix.

Here's why: experts in project management use a variety of metrics—performance to schedule, resource utilization, capital return rate, customer satisfaction, and many others. But if you study them closely, you'll find they're often used only in a backward-looking fashion to assess completed work. Sometimes that historical information gets incorporated into a future plan—as in "We got this result last time, so let's expect it again." But as with the other Task Types, too often project work is run without Really Useful Data, because typical project metrics don't automatically provide both of the two futures necessary—previous expectation versus current expectation.

What's the best way to represent project work with Really Useful Data? The question is especially important since managers often oversee a whole collection of projects that need to be summarized in a single graph.

Here's one possibility.

**Project Management**

Date: _____

| Project | Original Due Date | Current Forecast | Actual Delivery Date | 14 | 15 | 16 | 17 | 18 | 19 | 20 | 21 | 22 | 23 | 24 | 25 | 26 | 27 | 28 | 29 | 30 | 31 | 32 | 33 | 34 | Later |
|---|---|---|---|---|---|---|---|---|---|---|---|---|---|---|---|---|---|---|---|---|---|---|---|---|---|
| Project 1 | W42 | W43 | | | | | | | Deliverable | | | Deliverable | | | Deliverable | | | | Deliverable | | | | | | Deliverable |
| Project 2 | W42 | W42 | | | | | | | | | | Deliverable | | | Deliverable | | Deliverable | | | | | Deliverable | | |
| Project 3 | W42 | W42 | | | | Deliverable | | | | | Deliverable | | Deliverable | | | | | | | | Deliverable | | | |
| Project 4 | W42 | W44 | | | | | | | | | | | | | | Deliverable | | | Deliverable | | | | | Deliverable |
| Project 5 | W42 | W51 | | | | | Deliverable | | | | | | | Deliverable | | | Deliverable | | | | | Deliverable | | |
| Project 6 | W42 | W42 | | | | | | | | | | | Deliverable | | | Deliverable | | | | | Deliverable | | |
| Project 7 | W42 | W42 | | | Deliverable | | | | | | Deliverable | | Deliverable | | | | | Deliverable | | | | | |
| Project 8 | W42 | W42 | | | | | | | | | | | | | | | | Deliverable | | | | | |
| Project 9 | W34 | W34 | | | | | Deliverable | | | | | | Deliverable | | | Deliverable | | | Deliverable | Deliverable | Deliverable |
| Project 10 | W34 | W34 | | | | | | | | Deliverable | | Deliverable | | | | | Deliverable | | Deliverable | | | Deliverable | Deliverable |

Today

**KEY**
- On-track to complete on-time and within budget
- Caution: May miss commitment for scope, quality, time or budget
- Problem: Missed commitment certain or likely
- Completed

Each line in this table represents a different project, though you could also use the lines for parallel components of the same project. The columns are weeks, and the shaded squares are the points at which key deliverables or countable milestones are due. (In the final version, each instance of the word "deliverable" would be replaced with a short statement of actual output to be delivered.) The vertical line indicates today's date. So what you're looking for in this graph is ideally gray to the left and green to the right; everything that we thought would be finished is finished, and everything that we have coming up looks to be on schedule. That's how Project 1 looks.

Compare that to Project 5. We've completed all deliverables to date, but everything in the future is red, or likely to be missed. There's an issue here, even though the project is technically still on schedule at the moment. Now look at Project 10; it's also technically on schedule at the moment, but it's actually far ahead, with many future items already done. Could we move some Project 10 resources onto Project 5 to help it recover? And what about Project 7? We missed one deliverable, but we expect to be right on schedule going forward. This one would traditionally be labeled as behind, but there's no real issue needing attention here. It's certainly not in as much trouble as Project 5! This kind of data display drives attention toward the necessary resource allocation discussions and away from the unnecessary ones.

Consider an alternative approach to summarizing multiple projects.

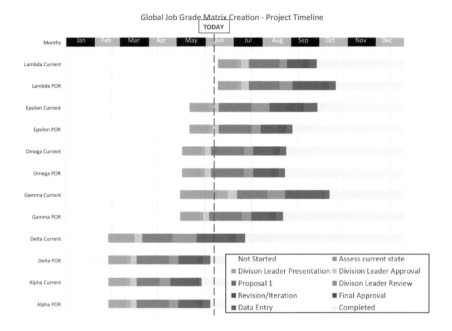

In this kind of display, we're dealing with a collection of projects, all of which have the same deliverables but with different time allocations to achieve them. Product releases, promotional campaigns, and process improvements are all examples of this. In this case, the specific output requirement is the final approval of a change proposal. You can see the outputs leading up to it: completion of current state assessment, presentation to division leader, approval by division leader, etc. Each horizontal block in the shaded bars represents the time needed to achieve the next sequential output.

Now, let's look at Lambda, the first of the collection. We're in June right now, and we're expecting to start our current state assessment within the next week. The second line for Lambda is the plan of record, or POR—what we originally planned. The first line is our current assessment of the future. As you can see, we've cut down our estimates for division leader review and revision (the green and dark blue sections), which has pulled in the expected completion date of "Current" relative to "POR" by almost a month.

Gamma, already underway, is a different story. We expected to be at the proposal writing stage by now—that's why the "Today" line crosses the blue section of the Gamma POR bar. But we're still finishing up the current state assessment; in the Gamma Current bar, the "Today" line crosses the orange section. We've also added time to our estimates for division leader review and revision; both the green and darker blue bars are longer in Current than they are in POR. Obviously, Gamma has been more challenging than expected. Whoever is waiting for this output to enable their own work had better plan on waiting longer, because our understanding of the future has changed.

These are only two examples of how to represent data for project-type tasks. You have many other options. There's no one perfect answer. But the key for projects is the same as the key for all other Task Types—to answer the question, how is it going to go differently than we expected? Hopefully this helps you think about how you track and report on your own project work.

# APPENDIX 5

## MANAGEMENT PRINCIPLES & GUIDANCE

Iterative Management is about behaviors, not labels. You don't need to define any terminology to start a useful conversation with your team that guides them toward a more Iterative approach. Consider sharing this summary of management principles to start the conversation with your management team.

**Management matters.**
Ours is consistent and coordinated. We do not accept the notion that everyone can manage as he or she sees fit. Our customers, products, and programs demand coordinated, intelligent decision-making and resource allocation; this requires that we work together in coordinated, intelligent management of the organization. Our management is a group activity, not an individual one.

**We're output focused.**
Effective results demand clarity of output. Managers at every level summarize planned results for themselves and each other as three to seven tangible output commitments. Constant communication and refinement of our abstracted measurable outputs is the foundation for decision-making and resource allocation; these commitments are the building block of trust between us.

**Our purpose is to allocate resources.**
Managers adjust resources to keep us on target. Management is our company's primary feedback system; its purpose is the constant realignment of

efforts and resources to move us as quickly as possible toward our goals. Customer, market, and technological reality change constantly; management's job is to ask what has changed, discover the answer, and adjust resourcing accordingly.

**We look forward.**
Everything we're trying to do is in the future. What are we trying to achieve in the future? How has our understanding of the future changed? Must we make adjustments based on that new understanding? These are the core questions of management, and they are fundamentally forward looking. History and current status are discussed only when pertinent to the future and how we might adjust resources in response to our new understanding of it.

**We work in teams on the leader's output.**
We succeed or fail together, not alone. We hold managers accountable for individual targets, but never at the expense of the organization. Every management team collaborates on its leader's output goals, and no individual has succeeded if the team has not. Managers debate decisions and share resources in pursuit of the higher-level goals for which they're held accountable.

**We encourage and demand realistic information.**
Killing messengers kills messages. The quality of our decisions and the intelligence of our actions are limited by the accuracy of our information. We reward truthful portrayals of all kinds and strictly prohibit any practice that deprioritizes accuracy in favor of palatability of the message. Bad news is good news because the sooner we get new information, the sooner we can respond.

**We meet regularly.**
The work of management is mostly done in meetings. We can't do alone what must be done together; we work individually but meet regularly to stay in lockstep. Only in our management meetings do we have the leverage to look across interrelated efforts in progress, comprehend changes on the horizon, and monitor and adjust our work so that we continue to hit our highest priority targets.

**We decide swiftly and act completely.**

Meetings are for decisions, not presentations. Decisions are set up by a short summary of objective, status, issue, and recommendation. We spend the majority of our time in the subsequent discussion, in which the decider learns as much as possible and then makes the best decision he or she can, irrespective of popularity or majority vote. We all implement fully whether or not we agree.

**We manage for a self-sufficient front line.**

The best forecasts come from our people. We ensure that our front line employees have clearly defined output goals, insight into their own progress, and maximum control over the resources they need. This enables them to predict their own output accurately, which leads to the truthful management forecasts we need to make resource allocation decisions at every level.

# RELATED READING

Academics and business experts alike have long been investigating how individuals, groups, and organizations go about arranging themselves, sharing information, making decisions, and developing and allocating resources as intelligent and flexible systems. While this reading list is by no means exhaustive—and while many of the entries below could arguably be added to more than one subcategory—each of the works listed here addresses some part of the question of how members of management can ensure that their organization is always taking the most intelligent step possible, based upon the most recent information available.

There is undoubtedly a chicken/egg dynamic in effect here. On the one hand, the works listed below provide the research and conceptual and anecdotal basis for Iterative Management. Some of them (including and especially *Change-ABLE Organization*) are central to the work, others (such as *A Complete Graphic Guide to Writing Smart as HELL Goals*) elaborate one particular aspect of it, and the rest provide supportive research and related ideas.

On the other hand, viewed through the lens of Iteration, these seven decades of work in sociology, psychology, organizational design, organizational behavior, neuroscience, and related fields coalesce into an integrated view of the purpose and function of management. Each one, in some way, fits with the notion that management's highest function is serving as a human feedback system whose purpose is optimal resource allocation.

Either way—whether the intent is to *come out* of these works with the concept of Iterative Management or to *go into* them with it in mind—the fact remains: once you understand it, the concept of Iterative Management is one of those things you can never "unsee."

## High-Performing and High-Efficiency Organizations

Balle, Michael, Daniel Jones, Jaques Chaize, and Orest Flume, *The Lean Strategy: Using Lean to Create Competitive Advantage, Unleash Innovation, and Deliver Sustainable Growth,* McGraw-Hill (2017).

Blanchard, Ken, *Leading at a Higher Level: Blanchard on Leadership and Creating High Performing Organizations,* FT Press (2006).

Collins, Jim, *Good to Great: Why Some Companies Make the Leap and Others Don't,* HarperCollins (2001).

Collins, Jim, and Jerry I. Porras, *Built to Last: Successful Habits of Visionary Companies,* HarperBusiness (1994).

Lencioni, Patrick, *The Advantage: Why Organizational Health Trumps Everything Else in Business,* Jossey-Bass (2012).

Likert, Rensis, *The Human Organization: Its Management and Value,* McGraw-Hill (1967).

Rummler, Geary A., and Alan P. Brache, *Improving Performance: How to Manage the White Space on the Organization Chart,* Jossey-Bass (1995).

Schein, Edgar, "Organizational Culture and Leadership" (1993), in *Classics of Organization Theory,* Jay Shafritz and J. Steven Ott (eds.), Harcourt College Publishers (2001).

Schmidt, Eric, and Jonathan Rosenberg, *How Google Works,* Grand Central Publishing (2017).

Senge, Peter, *The Fifth Discipline: The Art and Practice of the Learning Organization,* Doubleday (2006).

## Psychology and Sociology of Group Work

Asch, Solomon E., "Opinions and Social Pressure," *Scientific American* 193, no. 5 (1955).

Blakeslee, Sandra, "What Other People Say May Change What You See," *New York Times* (June 28, 2005).

Blass, Thomas, *The Man Who Shocked the World: The Life and Legacy of Stanley Milgram*, Basic Books (2004).

Fisher, Roger, William Ury, and Bruce Patton, *Getting to Yes: Negotiating Agreement without Giving In*, 2nd edition, Penguin Books (1991).

Hill, Gayle W., "Group Versus Individual Performance: Are N+1 Heads Better Than One?" *Psychological Bulletin* 91, no. 3 (1982).

Karpman, Stephen B., "Fairy Tales and Script Drama Analysis," *Transactional Analysis Bulletin* 7, no. 26 (1968).

Katz, Daniel, "Nationalism and Strategies of International Conflict Resolution," in *International Behavior: A Social Psychological Analysis*, H. C. Kelman (ed.), Holt, Rinehart and Winston (1965).

Lencioni, Patrick, *The Five Dysfunctions of a Team: A Leadership Fable*, Jossey-Bass (2002).

Milgram, Stanley, *Obedience to Authority*, Harper & Row (1974).

North, Douglass C., John Joseph Wallis, and Barry R. Weingast, *Violence and Social Orders: A Conceptual Framework for Interpreting Recorded Human History*, Cambridge University Press (2012).

Nutt, Paul C., *Why Decisions Fail: Avoiding the Blunders and Traps That Lead to Debacles*, Berrett-Koehler (2002).


## Individual Perception and Behavior

Csikszentmihalyi, Mihaly, *Flow: The Psychology of Optimal Experience*, Harper & Row (1990).

Demerouti, Evangelia, "Job Characteristics, Flow, and Performance: The Moderating Role of Conscientiousness," *Journal of Occupational Health Psychology* 11, no. 3 (2006).

Dilts, Robert B., and Judith A. Delozier, *Encyclopedia of Systemic Neuro-Linguistic Programming and NLP New Coding*, NLP University Press (2000).

Klein, Gary A., *How People Make Decisions*, 2nd edition, MIT Press (1999).

Marsten, William Moulton, *Emotions of Normal People*, Routledge (Reprinted 2001).

Rubenstein, J. S., D. E. Meyer, and J. E. Evans, "Executive Control of Cognitive Processes in Task Switching," *Journal of Experimental Psychology, Human Perception and Performance* 27, no. 4 (2001): 763–797.

Spranger, Eduard, *Types of Men*, Johnson Reprint Company (1966).

Surowiecki, James, "The Fatal-Flaw Myth," *The New Yorker* (July 31, 2006).

Zimbardo, Philip, *The Lucifer Effect: Understanding How Good People Turn Evil*, Random House (2008).

## Changing Individual Habits

Maurer, Robert, *One Small Step Can Change Your Life: The Kaizen Way*, Workman Publishing (2004).

Neal, David T., Wendy Wood, and Jeffrey M. Quinn, "Habits—a Repeat Performance," *Current Directions in Psychological Science* 15, no. 4 (2006).

Yin, Henry H., and Barbara J. Knowlton, "The Role of the Basal Ganglia in Habit Formation," *Nature Reviews Neuroscience* 7, no. 6 (2006).

## The Function of Management

Daniels, William R., *Change Able Organization*, ACT Publishing (1997).

Daniels, William R., *Group Power II: A Manager's Guide to Conducting Regular Meetings*, University Associates Inc. (1990).

Grove, Andrew S., *High Output Management*, Random House (1985).

Katz, Daniel, and Robert L. Kahn, *The Social Psychology of Organizations*, Wiley (1966).

## The Function of Managing

Daniels, William R., *Breakthrough Performance Managing for Speed and Flexibility*, ACT Publishing (1995).

Hughes, Glenn, *A Graphic Guide to Writing Smart as HELL Goals*, Smart as Hell (2015).

Wilson, Clark L., *How and Why Effective Managers Balance Their Skills*, Clark Wilson (2003).

## The Function of Change Management

Bridges, William, *Managing Transitions*, William Bridges and Associates (1991–2009).

Cook, Sarah, Steve Macaulay, and Hilary Coldicott, *Change Management Excellence: Using the Four Intelligences for Successful Organizational Change*, Kogan Page (2004).

Kegan, Robert, and Lisa Laskow Lahey, *Immunity to Change: How to Overcome It and Unlock the Potential in Yourself and Your Organization*, Harvard Business School Press (2009).

## The Function of Leadership

DePaul, Gary A., *Nine Practices of 21st Century Leadership: A Guide for Inspiring Creativity, Innovation, and Engagement*, CRC Press (2016).

Kouzes, James M., and Barry Z. Posner, *The Leadership Challenge: How to Make Extraordinary Things Happen in Organizations*, 6th edition, Wiley (2017).

## Development of Human Capability

Goldsmith, Marshall, *What Got You Here Won't Get You There: How Successful People Become Even More Successful*, Hachette Books (2007).

Goleman, Daniel, *Social Intelligence: The New Science of Human Relationships*, Bantam Books (2006).

Goleman, Daniel, *Working with Emotional Intelligence*, Bantam Books (1998).

Kegan, Robert, *The Evolving Self: Problem and Process in Human Development*, Harvard University Press (1982).

Stanier, Michael Bungay, *The Coaching Habit: Say Less, Ask More & Change the Way You Lead Forever*, Box of Crayons Press (2016).


## Understanding and Changing Culture

Muzio, Edward, *Make Work Great*, McGraw-Hill (2010).

Schneider, William E., *The Reengineering Alternative: A Plan for Making Your Current Culture Work*, McGraw-Hill Professional (1994).

Shafritz, Jay, and J. Steven Ott, eds., *Classics of Organization Theory*, Harcourt (2001).

Trompenaars, Alfons, *Riding the Waves of Culture: Understanding Cultural Diversity in Business*, Irwin Professional Publishers (1993–1997).


## Related Concepts from Neuroscience

Engel, Andreas K., Pascal Fries, and Wolf Singer, "Dynamic Predictions: Oscillations and Synchrony in Top-Down Processing," *Nature Reviews Neuroscience* 2, no. 10 (2001): 704–716.

Gloor, Peter, and Scott Cooper, "The New Principles of a Swarm Business," *MIT Sloan Management Review* 48, no. 3 (2007): 81.

Heylighen, Francis, "Stigmergy as a Universal Coordination Mechanism: Components, Varieties and Applications," in *Human Stigmergy: Theoretical Developments and New Applications*, T. Lewis and L. Marsh (eds.), Springer (in publication).

Poldrack, Russell A., and Mark G. Packard, "Competition Among Multiple Memory Systems: Converging Evidence from Animal and Human Brain Studies," *Neuropsychologia* 41, no. 3 (2003): 245–251.

Roli, Andrea, Marco Villani, Alessandro Filisetti, and Roberto Serra, "Dynamical Criticality: Overview and Open Questions," arXiv: 1512.05259 [nlin.AO] (2015). Accessed from Cornell University Libraries at https://arxiv.org/abs/1512.05259.

Starter, Martin, Ben Givens, and John P. Bruno, "The Cognitive Neuroscience of Sustained Attention: Where Top-Down Meets Bottom-Up," *Brain Research Reviews* 35, no. 2 (2001): 146–160.

Tummolini, L., and C. Castelfranchi, "Trace Signals: The Meanings of Stigmergy," in *Environments for Multi-Agent Systems III: E4MAS 2006*, D. Weyns, H. V. D. Parunak, and F. Michel (eds.), Lecture Notes in Computer Science 4389, Springer (2007): 141–156.

Van Dyke Parunak, H., "A Survey of Environments and Mechanisms for Human-Human Stigmergy," in *Environments for Multi-Agent Systems II*, D. Weyns, H. V. D. Parunak, and F. Michel (eds.), Springer (2006): 163–186.

Van Dyke Parunak, H., et al. "Stigmergic Modeling of Hierarchical Task Networks," in *Multi-Agent-Based Simulation X: MABS 2009*, G. Di Tosto, H. Van Dyke Parunak (eds.), Lecture Notes in Computer Science 5683, Springer (2010): 98–109.

Waldrop, M. Mitchell, "The Trillion Dollar Vision of Dee Hock," *Fast Company* (October 31, 1996).

# INDEX

# ABOUT THE AUTHOR

Ed Muzio's mantra is "higher output, lower stress, sustainable growth." He is CEO of Group Harmonics and author of *Make Work Great* and *Four Secrets to Liking Your Work*. Both books won Awards of Excellence from the International Society for Performance Improvement, a professional association that requires both a clear problem statement and a measurable result for organizational performance improvements.

Ed has been called "one of the planet's clearest thinkers on management practice" by someone who would know, the editor of an international management magazine. He is a leader in the application of analytical models to group and organizational effectiveness and output—including whole-group intervention, simulation, facilitation, and instructional design. Originally trained as an engineer, Ed has started organizations large and small, led global initiatives in technology development and employee recruitment, and published articles and refereed papers ranging from manufacturing strategy to the relationships between individual skills and output.

Ed's work on organizational culture has been hailed as producing measurable results even in the most difficult circumstances. His analytical approach to human productivity has been featured in national and international media, including CBS News, Fox Business News, and the *New York Post*; he has been a regular contributor to CBS, Monster.com, and the *Huffington Post*. With clients ranging from individual life coaches to Fortune 500 companies, he serves as an adviser and educator to professionals at all levels, all over the world.

Prior to founding Group Harmonics in 2004, Ed was president and executive director of a human services organization and a leader, mentor, and technologist within Intel Corporation and the Sematech consortium. A Cornell University graduate, Ed's accomplishments include the creation and stewardship of a worldwide manufacturing infrastructure program, a nationally recognized engineering development organization, and a nonprofit residential program serving at-risk youth in his hometown of Albuquerque, New Mexico. Ed lives in Austin, Texas, with his wife and son.